Survival of

American Democracy:

Virtual Reality vs. Actual Reality, a Metaphor, and the Irony of Christianity

by

Bruce P. Burns, Ph.D., Clinical Psychologist

Proctor Publications, LLC, Ann Arbor, Michigan

Library of Congress Catalog Number: 96–68693

Publisher's Cataloging in Publication
(Prepared by Quality Books Inc.)

Burns, Bruce P.
Survival of American Democracy : virtual reality vs. actual reality, a metaphor, and the irony of Christianity / by Bruce P. Burns.
p.cm.
Includes bibliographical references and indexes.
ISBN: 1–882792–25–4 paper
ISBN: 1–882792–30–0 cloth

1. Democracy–United States. 2. Democracy–Moral and ethical aspects. 3. United States–Politics and government. 4. Religion and state. 5. Christianity and politics. I. Title.

JC423.B87 1996 320.973
QBI96–40144

Printed in the United States of America

Dedicated to:

Grant Erik Burns

my beloved twin brother
who is senior to me in every positive way
(God's strength is made perfect in weakness)

Acknowledgment To:

Paula

Who helped me edit this manuscript and also who provided invaluable comments. Thank you for keeping me focused, and for your constant constructive support and encouragement. You were indispensable and have my deepest appreciation and admiration.

Table of Contents

Preface

It is commonly written and stated, in this closing time of the twentieth century, that Americans must put into everyday life more moral and ethical values! The symptoms of a very sick society are increasingly all around us. It is my belief that the United States of America will, once again, be the beacon of democracy, the symbol of freedom, hope and respect for every individual, upon the return to and the practice of: the Koran, the Torah and the Bible by the Muslims, the Jews and the Christians, but not by their fanatical fringes (read: intolerant and/or militant factions). Because I am a Christian, it is from this viewpoint that I write this book.

Today especially, with all the crime, drugs, family break-ups, job insecurity and world tensions, people need help to learn how to cope and to survive in this world. More and more, it becomes increasingly apparent that we need God's love and strength, which only comes through a living faith that is so often lacking in nominal Christians. At this point, I am still a sinner, but also a believer, pinning all my hope in God's love and the work of Jesus Christ.

Thus, this is a book written about faith and the life of faith by one still struggling with sin. I think that many other believers struggle in similar ways. I do not believe we are 'perfected' before the Messiah's return and I do believe many struggle with this issue of doubting whether they have faith or can, indeed, even be saved because of the ongoing sin in their lives. I feel it is important to remove this roadblock from the lives of believers so that they can move ahead and get on with leading a life that is growing in its demonstration of faith, instead of stagnating in doubt.

There is a growing 'angst' today that is a product of accretion from living as though God and injustices were really not understandable and, therefore, consigning such 'things' to limbo. The resulting loss of ultimate meaning and overarching purpose to human life leaves an emptiness that is more like a spacelessness. Even in many American's worship, God does not play a vital or real part. Deep thought and worship is not often given to ultimate reality and what comes after death. The surmise that nothing follows death and, therefore, one had better get the 'full' of living now, could be responsible for much of the selfishness of modern life and fear of death. On the other hand, if one thinks that perhaps there is some kind of hereafter for the individual, but denial or repression consigns any further search, seeking or thought to a memory cell marked 'do not open', the result could be a ticking time-bomb of dread. The coffin of death is often viewed as a 'Pandora's box' which is best left closed. Modern man needs to lift that lid and make a studied inquiry into what lies inside. Otherwise, he lives with a growing sense of meaninglessness that turns some to cynicism and others to despair, but always underneath is a growing sense of anxiety that slowly turns to dread. This book is about overcoming this 'angst' by lifting the repression caused by the apparent irony* of Christian preaching and Christian living. Now, in this age of VIRTUAL REALITY, we can, if we want, understand Jesus Christ in a way that allows the gift of God, i.e., faith, to open our eyes, ears, minds, hearts and souls, to **ACTUAL REALITY** and thus become receptive to His love.

*"In a general sense, irony marks a lack of accordance between what is uttered and what is meant, yet in such a way that the door is left ajar for people to get an inkling of what the speaker or writer actually means. Because it is not possible to expound Christianity directly, nor to preach about ethical conduct, because both presuppose that the preacher reduplicates his preaching [practices what he preaches]; but who can say about himself that he fulfills the claims of Christianity or even of ethics?"[10](*The Diary of Soren Kierkegaard*. 1960: Philosophical Library, Inc., New York. Translated from the Danish by Gerda M. Andersen. Edited by Peter P. Rohde. Page 231, section 144)
"I don't know Who – or what – put the question, I don't know when it was put. I don't even remember answering. But at some moment I did answer YES to Someone – or Something – and from that hour I was certain that existence is meaningful and that, therefore, my life, in self-surrender, had a goal."[6] (*Markings* by Dag Hammarskjold)[See page 90.]

Disclaimer

This book is not meant to offend any child of GOD, nor is it to be reflective of judgment of any other person on my part. I am a Christian and so the book is written from that perspective; however, if it sounds as though I am passing some kind of judgmental damnation on any non-Christian, please refer to this Disclaimer and re-orient your mind to dismiss that error and continue reading.

After all, Jews, Muslims, as well as Christians, all have Abraham as their spiritual father. Furthermore, Buddhists, Confucianists, and Hindus, along with other organized religions, may very well be received by God and have entrance into His Actual Reality, for Christ said,

"Judge not, that ye be not judged." (Matthew 7:1) And, *"Let not your heart be troubled: ye believe in God, believe also in Me. In My Father's house are many mansions: if it were not so, I would have told you. I go to prepare a place for you."* (John 14:1-2) And, *"For when the Gentiles, which have not the law, do by nature the things contained in the law, these, having not the law, are a law unto themselves."* (Romans 2:14)

Therefore, please, when I have transgressed your beliefs or have offended you who are not a Christian, again, please refer to this Disclaimer.

Introduction

Striving to make your faith real is worthy of a lifetime's effort of whatever length the Lord assigns you. It is emphasized in these pages that faith is the basic tenet of Christianity. It is my belief that the purpose of a human being is to get back to a position wherein God is his or her center and he or she is in a living relationship with Him. As a Christian, I believe this is only possible through Jesus Christ with the empowerment of the Holy Spirit. One big hurdle, I believe, is that, in general, the Bible is not understood and, therefore, not read. Or if it is read, it is done so mostly as a ritual and with little interest or understanding. This, of course, does not refer to everybody nor to all churches, but it is too often true. It is my understanding that we may be 'born again', but I believe that most of us are not able to fully become 'sons' and 'daughters' of God while we are physically on earth. That is, not until after we are resurrected upon Christ's return in glory. Our sojourn on earth is to become eligible for resurrection and to avoid the 'second death'. In one sense, we are only in the *process of becoming* the 'children' of God while alive.

These statements and everything in this book, except for quotations from direct scripture and from other authors, are my opinions and beliefs. In no way do I claim that these have been revealed to me, nor that I speak with authority. Although if any truth resides in this book, it is from inspiration by the Holy Spirit. But within these pages, or if at all in any of the pages, truth does exist, I do not know, except as a matter of my own personal faith. So we are, again, constantly thrown back upon our own to seek individual inspiration and guidance from God's Holy Spirit. I can only pray that my thoughts are heuristic and will help others to come to the knowledge of the truth. All scriptural quotations, unless otherwise stated, are from the King James version of the Bible of 1611. The reader may find it helpful to purchase the New King James Version (NKJV). It is somewhat easier reading because the archaic forms of our language have been brought up to date and yet it is still an accurate rendition of the original. The terms man, son, him, etc., are more to be used as generic in this book as opposed to sexist. I did this because it is awkward and, at times, stops the flow of thought to constantly be saying he/she, him/her, man/woman, etc.

There are so many mysteries in the Bible, one of the intriguing ones being that of the two creations in Genesis. The Bible does say (in the 'first creation') that 'man' refers to male and female and were created at the same time; in the 'second creation', man is the head of the woman and God is the head of man. It seems to me that 'man' and 'woman' are only assigned aspects of humans in this life, but in the immortal hereafter for 'believers' and 'saints', we are once again co-equal. Saint Peter, speaking of and to women, "*But let it be the **hidden man of the heart**, in that which is not corruptible, even the ornament of a meek and quiet spirit, which is in the sight of God of great price.*" (1 Peter 3:4) Christianity elevates woman far above any other religion and directs the husband to honor the wife. Women played an important part throughout the Bible. In the first creation, man and woman were created at the same time and were equal; in the second creation, woman was taken out of man who preceded her. It is interesting to note that in the 'final' purely human stage of man (that is before the time of Revelation when non-human agents play a publicly visible part), God, in His earthly manifestation, 'came through' woman so to speak in the form of Jesus Christ being born of the Virgin Mary.

Evolution and psychology have to do with carnal knowledge and do not lead to an understanding of God and Spiritual reality. In creation, idea precedes structure and function. Essence precedes physical manifestation or existence. The essence of man and woman was created by God, but it was a creation outside of time (as we know it) and will survive beyond time. Humans have the choice of becoming immortal spiritual beings (**ACTUAL REALITY**), or remaining time-trapped in a physical body and a carnal mind (VIRTUAL REALITY). For present-day, technical descriptions of 'virtual reality', which is the basis for the analogy used throughout this book, you may refer to articles in *Newsweek* (2/27/95) and *Time* (Spring 1995). Other examples of virtual reality, in the sense of an appearance of reality, would be photographs, mirror reflections, shadows, silhouettes, compact discs, television images, motion pictures, and stage plays. These are all representations or reproductions of 'real' things or life.

Similarly, but at a different level, would be a phantom limb (the feeling of pain in a limb that has been amputated). Illusions of varying degrees are performed by magicians, often very convincingly, even though you know it is not reality. In 'sick' or psychotic minds, delusions and hallucinations can exist, which are unshakable in the face of opposing evidence, facts or reality. It is my hypothesis or argument in this book that our human, earthly 'reality' is in fact only an appearance of reality, in other words VIRTUAL REALITY. This is an 'hypnotic' illusion so strongly held that, in effect, the natural (carnal) mind is deluded about the nature and reality of things, which I refer to as **ACTUAL REALITY**. As the Bible expresses it, *"For now we see through a glass, darkly; but then face to face: now I know in part; but then shall I know even as also I am known."* (1 Corinthians 13:12) *"Whereas ye know not what shall be on the morrow. For what is your life? It is even a vapour, that appeareth for a little time, and then vanisheth away."* (James 4:14) *"Beloved, now are we the sons of God, and it doth not yet appear what we shall be: but we know that, when He shall appear, we shall be like Him; for we shall see Him as He is."* (1 John 3:2) This applies mainly to Christians but not, I believe, to Christians in name only.

At some point after their creation, earthly humans chose to disobey God and they ate of the 'forbidden fruit'. Their choice was between good and evil. The choice itself was evil; it was against God's will that they chose to 'know' evil and to 'know' is to experience. In other words, they were not content with good. They either wanted to satisfy their curiosity or to disobey (be independent of) God – or both. Obviously, evil existed prior to the physical creation of humans, but humans were in some way immune to it or unaffected by it until their disobedience. Evil is adversity and humans became enmeshed in it from that point on. From Adam and Eve on, humans have had to continually choose, and so far, except for Jesus Christ, no one (with two possible exceptions, Enoch and Elijah) has consistently chosen 'good'. In fact, things have gotten to such a point that, at times, it seems impossible to know what is the 'good' or the right choice. Even when this isn't the case, some humans deliberately choose evil. One must constantly ask and believe that he receives guidance (subtle and often hidden) from the Holy Spirit. This comes with the acceptance of and obedience to Jesus Christ. God provides us with whatever will, motivation, intelligence, character and strength needed to being so guided.

We are, as a society, in a pagan-like phase. I hope it is a phase America will pass out of and, once again, become a beacon of freedom and Christianity to the world for a long time into the future. It is my hope as a human and as a clinical psychologist that this book will help complete the 'therapeutic' process of my profession, with the necessary work of an on-going faith. It is my belief that in this re-direction of efforts, with its emphasis in the arena of Christian faith, the real 'healing' occurs. America is sorely in need of a healing. It is as if Americans have lost a sense of unity, loyalty and pride in their country. The real roots of America lie not only in giving equal opportunity to all, but in being true to our heritage which, in a large part, is derived from Biblical faith. Mr. Evan's book *The Theme is Freedom* [3] gives some revealing insights into this aspect. To quote from Newt Gingrich's book, *To Renew America*, "Multiculturalism switched the emphasis from proclaiming allegiance to the common culture to proclaiming the virtues (real or imagined) of a particular ethnicity, sect, or tribe. 'Situational ethics' and 'deconstructionism' – the belief that there are no general rules of behavior – began to supplant the centuries-old struggle to establish universal standards of right and wrong."(Page 30)

If the Bible can be made more intelligible and, thus, more interesting simply by calling attention to its profound statements in a way applicable to everyday life, this book will have achieved its purpose. This is a book written by a sinner for sinners (we are the ones Jesus came to earth to save) who have the hope of Heaven because of Jesus Christ, and Him crucified, but risen from the grave victorious over death, sin and Satan, and coming back for us.

Chapter 1
Corruption of Reality

If you think man is inherently good, please let your eyes be opened. All through history, men have been slaughtering each other or enslaving others in one way or another. Imagine what kind of an adult a baby would grow into if he were never trained or disciplined. When God created man as male and female, for the first time, in their essence, they were perfect – like God. *"So God created man in His Own image, in the image of God created He him; male and female created He them."* (Genesis 1:27) Later, He actually formed natural man into physical existence. *"And the Lord God formed man of the dust of the ground, and breathed into his nostrils the breath of life; and man became a living soul."* (Genesis 2:7) And, shortly after that, He formed woman. *"And the Lord God caused a deep sleep to fall upon Adam, and he slept: and He took one of his ribs, and closed up the flesh instead thereof; And the rib, which the Lord God had taken from man, made He a woman, and brought her unto the man."* (Genesis 2:21-22)

Now, this natural or earthy male and female were not perfect, not inherently good, because as soon as God had formed man, He gave him a commandment, *"And the Lord God commanded the man, saying, Of every tree of the garden thou mayest freely eat: But of the tree of the knowledge of good and evil, thou shalt not eat of it: for in the day that thou eatest thereof thou shalt surely die."* (Genesis 2:16-17) So here we can understand St. Paul in Romans when he refers to sin dwelling in him. Sin was in man, but he would not have known it if it were not for God's commandment (refer to Romans 7:14-25). Thus, can we not assume that when God translated man from his essence to his existence on the physical plane (from spiritual to natural), He gave this new creation the opportunity to fail or disobey, i.e., freedom?

There are some things we don't understand about man: freedom, creation, good and evil. We need not blind ourselves to this forever. In a four-dimensional, physical world we are time-trapped AND are not 'as gods'. Christ came down and demonstrated how the essence of 'perfect' man would be on the physical, four-dimensional plane. I believe that God's **ACTUAL REALITY** is non-dimensional; it is **being** without boundaries of time and space. Thus, God said, "*. . . I AM THAT I AM*" (Exodus 3:14) and Jesus said, "*. . . I Am.*" (John 8:58) In our VIRTUAL REALITY, we have four dimensions in which we must progress from becoming to **Being**. Adam failed, you and I were then doomed to failure. Christ succeeded and empowers us to succeed. We can choose to try to be the 'greatest' here on earth and then to die and perish (be damned to being less than our real essence, and perhaps knowing it for the rest of eternity) or choose to become spiritually minded, rejecting the carnal mind, so that when our natural or earthy body is set aside, we can be translated into immortality with Almighty God and Jesus Christ. Once again, listen to St. Paul, *"The Spirit itself beareth witness with our spirit, that we are the children of God: And if children, then heirs; heirs of God, and joint-heirs with Christ, if so be that we suffer with Him, that we may be also glorified together. For I reckon that the sufferings of this present time are not worthy to be compared with the glory which shall be revealed in us."* (Romans 8:16-18)

It really goes against the grain of puffed up human egos to admit that their only hope of immortality is through humility, faith and love! The way that St. Paul puts it, *"For the Jews require a sign, and the Greeks seek after wisdom: But we preach Christ crucified, unto the Jews a stumbling block, and unto the Greeks foolishness; But unto them which are called, both Jews and Greeks, Christ the power of God, and the wisdom of God. Because the foolishness of God is wiser than men; and the weakness of God is stronger than men."* (1 Corinthians 1:22-25) Just look at the world scene; men never get enough money or power or fame or possessions. What a corruption man's reality or VIRTUAL REALITY (see page 61) is of God's **ACTUAL REALITY**. Look at leaders such as Hitler and Napoleon. The only things that make a human being enduringly happy are spiritual gifts, and these come only from God through Jesus Christ via the Holy Spirit. Furthermore, this is the only route to make others genuinely happy, especially loved ones.

Perhaps you have had the experience of believing in God and Jesus as a child, and then later, in high school, college or as an adult, no longer believing. It seems that everything in modern day life conspires to break down that child-like faith we had. Who among us with our 'sophistication' and awareness of psychology, evolution and the modern day scientific achievements can or would even want to maintain that child-like faith? We may go through the motions and the lip service either for the benefit of our children or simply as a social resource. Yet Christ said, "*Verily I say unto you, Except ye be converted, and become as little children, ye shall not enter into the kingdom of heaven.*" (Matthew 18:3) Does it strike you as strange that it is so difficult to maintain a child-like faith as an adult? It really is quite amazing how so many adults can call themselves Christians and ignore the plain statements of the New Testament. St. Paul said, "*But without faith it is impossible to please Him: for he that cometh to God must believe that He is, and that He is a rewarder of them that diligently seek Him.*" (Hebrews11:6) Here is a basic tenet of Christianity, you must believe! The choice is yours. Faith is a gift from God, (just as college tuition is a gift from a father to his child, but the child must work for the degree), available to all who hear the message. If you hear it, you have been called! Called[†] to believe, and then welcomed to ask of God for further guidance and spiritual gifts.

There is a maturing process wherein the constant presence and love of God is increasingly felt. This maturing comes about through prayer and through a growing sensitivity to how the Holy Spirit wants you to be, all of which is accessed through reading the New Testament. Why do you suppose it is so hard to establish or to maintain your Christian faith? Because the natural man is opposed to 'losing himself' or 'denying' himself. Natural man corrupts the entire process, reversing the notion of denying self and striving to promote self and to be self-seeking. Another way of saying to lose your 'self' is to become 'other' directed, but with a difference. This is such a key point that Oswald Chambers[1] expressed so eloquently that I am devoting the next several paragraphs to quoting from his book, *Biblical Psychology*, pages 134-136.

"We have defined love, in its highest sense, as being the sovereign preference of my person for another person. The surest sign that God has done a work of grace in my heart is that I love Jesus Christ best, not weakly and faintly, not intellectually, but passionately, personally and devotedly, overwhelming every other love of my life.

"In Romans 5:5, '. . .*because the love of God is shed abroad in our hearts by the Holy Ghost which is given unto us'*, Paul does **not** say that the **capacity** to love God is shed abroad in our hearts, he says *'the **love of God** is shed abroad.'* The Bible knows only one love in this connection, and that is the supreme, dominating love of God. Jesus Christ teaches that if we have had a work of grace done in our hearts, we will show to our fellow men the same love God has shown to us. *'A new commandment I give unto you, That ye love one another; as I have loved you, that ye also love one another.'* (John 13:34)

"The natural heart, we cannot repeat it too often, does not want the Gospel. We will take God's blessings and His loving-kindnesses and prosperity, but when it comes to close quarters and God's Spirit informs us that we have to give up the rule of ourselves and let Him rule us, then we understand what Paul means when he says the 'carnal mind' (which resides in the heart) 'is enmity against God.' Are we willing for God not to suppress or counteract, but to totally alter the ruling disposition of our heart? The wonderful work of the grace of God is that through the Atonement God can alter the centre of my life, and put there a supreme, passionate devotion to God Himself.

"The natural man does not like God's commands; he will not have them, he covers them over and ignores them. Jesus said that the first commandment is '. . .*thou shalt love the Lord thy God with all thy heart, and with all thy soul, and with all thy mind, and with all thy strength:. . .'*. (Mark 12:30) Men put the second commandment first, '. . .*Thou shalt love thy neighbour as thyself. . .'* The great cry today is 'love for mankind'. The great cry of Jesus is 'love God first,' and this love, the highest love, the supreme, passionate devotion of the life, springs from the inner centre.

"What a rest comes when the love of God has been shed abroad in my heart by the Holy Spirit! I realize that God is love, not loving, but **love**, something infinitely greater than loving, consequently He has to be very stern. There is no such thing as God overlooking sin. That is where people make a great mistake with regard to love; they say, 'God is love and, of course, He will forgive sin:' God is holy love and He cannot forgive sin. Jesus Christ did not come to forgive sin; He came to **save** us from our sins. The salvation of Jesus Christ removes the 'sinner' out of my heart and plants in the 'saint'. That is the marvelous work of God's grace.

"That the natural heart of man does not want the Gospel of God is proved by the resentment of the heart against the working of the Spirit of God, 'No, I don't object to being forgiven, I don't mind being guided and blessed, but it is too much of a radical surrender to ask me to **give up my right to myself** and allow the Spirit of God to have absolute control of my heart.' That is the natural resentment. But oh, the ineffable, unspeakable delight when we are made one with God, one with Jesus Christ, and one with every fellow-believer in this great, overwhelming characteristic of love, when life becomes possible on God's plan!"[1]

I do believe that the foregoing paragraph describes a 'saint' as per my description in chapter 6, for I have not experienced this 'giving up my right to myself' yet and I hope that is because it is a growth process and I am still struggling with my self, and if I should die in this stage, I would hope that Christ's work will have 'saved me' from sin, even though 'as by fire'. I believe that God first puts His love in your heart (thereafter, your asking and wanting and receiving it occurs), i.e., He first loves you and then, when you recognize it and accept it, you **begin** to feel it and you become able to love Him back, and increasingly able to love your fellow man. Constantly beset upon by Satan in the form of doubt about God or that you have been accepted by God, these doubts plus your inability to be 'perfect' or anywhere near that in being loving toward others, is an on-going struggle – at least it is in my life.

God is constantly empowering us to "*. . .live, and move, and have our being. . .*" (Acts 17:28) in Him. He is the source of all creativity and productivity, i.e., of all essence and all existence. *"For it is God which worketh in you both to will and to do of His good pleasure."* (Philippians 2:13) He has placed us in a physical world with the potential of becoming spiritual beings. There are two forces from which we can constantly choose, one carnal and the other spiritual. The former is time-trapped and subject to death as a finality. The latter is immortal and in constant relationship with God, and can only be brought about through the intervention of His Son, Jesus Christ. We need to acknowledge our helplessness and utter dependence upon God. It is necessary that we give up ourselves to God's Holy Spirit in order to be fruitful in this physical world and to carry out His will. We are nothing in and of ourselves. All glory, all power is His. He has satisfied and reconciled His love with His justice toward us. This has been achieved, through His grace, by the sacrifice of His Son, Jesus Christ, for our sins.

Those of us who have been called from the beginning of the World as His, may accept His gift of faith, as that is what it is. It is nothing we earned or deserved. But without faith, it is impossible to please God, as the scripture states. Do you know whether you have been called? It is very important that you do know and to accept this gift of faith, and then to walk in it. For as the New Testament states, *"For many are called, but few are chosen."* (Matthew 22:14) You may be plagued with doubts whether God has called you and whether you will be accepted. So your first task is to determine whether you have been called, i.e., graced with faith, and second, it is your task to walk in your faith. The mere fact that you wonder and are concerned whether or not you have been called or selected, is verification that you have received this gift of being called[†], and therefore, have a valid and legitimate hope of being chosen. Furthermore, you can begin to demonstrate that great gift of faith. *"For by grace are ye saved through faith; and that not of yourselves: it is the gift of God. Not of works, lest any man should boast."* (Ephesians 2:8) *"So then faith cometh by hearing, and hearing by the word of God."* (Romans 10:17) *"He that is of God heareth God's words. . ."* (John 8:47) *"Examine yourselves, whether ye be in the faith; prove your own selves. . ."* (2 Corinthians 13:5)

It is less a question of asking why but of how, and then of 'walking' step by faltering step, seeking guidance by the Holy Spirit – just 'feeling' your way along. However, I believe, it is most vital to keep certain instructions in mind, such as:

1. Do not judge others, whether or not they believe differentlyor see things differently than you;
2. Keep on doing whatever vocation you had when you realized you were called, unless you receive guidance to change your work or way of life. If you do, it will become stronger and stronger in your mind. God will have His way with you if you are receptive and obedient to the best of your ability;
3. Pray and seek Him progressively, but in private;
4. You are to be in the world but not of it, reject carnal thinking and desires;
5. God will deal with you spiritually, your needs will be taken care of; but if you suffer, remember, Christ suffered and you are open to taking His afflictions upon yourself;
6. The blessings you will be given are spiritual and priceless, such as joy, peace, love, faith, patience, humility, temperance, brotherly love, godliness, goodness, gentleness, kindness;
7. All things that happen to you are for your good, no matter how they appear;
8. Above all, let the love of God into your heart and let it flow from you to everyone;
9. Be part of a Christ-centered community;*

10. First allegiance to God, second to family, third to community.

Many schools of psychology use a concept called the 'unconscious' to 'explain' why we do bad things. Quite opposed to this is the concept that we, in effect, are **receptors**. That is, we either act upon positive guidance coming to us from God or negative guidance coming from Satan. When we deny this spiritual element, we rationalize to account for man's genius or diabolicalness. However, when we do this, we may either elevate man to supplant God or we may become unwitting pawns of the devil. In either case, we center on ourselves, usually either becoming puffed up with self or confused. Thus, the biblical admonition from Christ, who said, "... *If any man will come after Me, let him deny himself, and take up his cross and follow Me."* (Matthew 16:24) He also said, *"I am the way, the truth, and the life: no man cometh unto the Father, but by Me."* (John 14:6)

Once you can accept that God has called you, through Christ, and that in His grace He has freely blessed you with the gift of faith, special things begin to happen in your heart and your mind. You find that you can accept this gift, despite the awareness of your unworthiness, in fact, largely because of your unworthiness (you didn't earn it or deserve it, so it had to be a gift). This allows you to begin to understand that He chose you, in the sense of calling you. Once you absorb that He loved you first, long before you ever loved Him, you begin to 'feel' how great and wonderful is His love and how it begins to change you, empowering you to become more loving. Your heart 'opens up' so to speak; you become 'softer'. Empathy and compassion grow while judgmentalness and negativism decline. Now, the spiritual gifts loom more and more attractive (love, peace, joy, faith, etc.) and it becomes easier to see and to reject carnal things, such as youth and physical beauty, riches and power, as ends in and of themselves, all time-bound and transitory.

Once you 'know' that God does love you, through Christ,

your love for Him grows. You begin to understand what St. Paul meant when he said, *"And we know that all things work together for good to them that love God, to them who are the called according to His purpose."* (Romans 8:28) When we pray and when we try to heed the Holy Spirit, we find that we fail so often that we must realize that it is 'sin' in us and not we ourselves in our spiritual minds. If we don't understand this, we get discouraged or even begin to feel that we don't have faith (haven't been called). St. Paul addresses this area of concern, *"For we know that the law is spiritual: but I am carnal, sold under sin. For that which I do I allow not: for what I would, that do I not; but what I hate, that do I. If then I do that which I would not, I consent unto the law that it is good. Now then it is no more I that do it, but sin that dwelleth in me. For I know that in me (that is, in my flesh,) dwelleth no good thing: for to will is present with me; but how to perform that which is good I find not. For the good that I would I do not: but the evil which I would not, that I do. Now if I do that I would not, it is no more I that do it, but sin that dwelleth in me. I find then a law, that, when I would do good, evil is present with me."* (Romans 7:14-21) To help clarify the foregoing, take as an example any kind of addiction (smoking, alcohol, drugs, pornography, etc.). One reaches the point where they wish to rid themselves of being in the grip of a habit, compulsion, addiction or obsession and yet the individual cannot break the enslavement. In fact, often the more effort one makes it seems the more one becomes controlled by the substance, pre-occupation or activity. This would indicate that when we pray, it must be with a spiritual mind. So the world or man's so-called reality is opposed to and tries to corrupt God's Reality, which I call **ACTUAL REALITY**.

Jesus Christ said, *"Ask, and it shall be given you; seek, and ye shall find; knock, and it shall be opened unto you:"* (Matthew 7:7) The more you pray (not by rote or superstitiously) the more your sense of awe toward God grows. It drives home to you how much God has been with you, protecting and blessing you, forgiving you, waiting for you to let Him come into your heart with that sense of peace and security, warmth and love. This grows slowly and gradually and is nurtured by prayer in a subtle way. (Refer to Untermeyer[16], page 1002, Francis Thompson's poem, *The Hound of Heaven*, which illustrates how 'man' seeks every 'reality' except God's and yet God doesn't give up on 'man', the Hound of Heaven representing Christ.) We are in this world but not of it, as St. John states, *"Love not the world, neither the things that are in the world. If any man love the world, the love of the Father is not in him. For all that is in the world, the lust of the flesh, and the lust of the eyes, and the pride of life, is not of the Father, but is of the world."* (1 John 2:15-16)

*Community defined as a relationship – not organization – of believers (in the New Testament sense as spelled out in this book). It may be among nearby residents, i.e. more or less neighbors of the same city, village or township, and/or over long-distance by means of letters, telephone, radio or computer. It is to be the body of Christ – not the glory of men. There are no edifices or formal structures for meetings, only 'get togethers' in homes or open spaces. No hierarchy of officers or leaders. No contentiousness, disputes or arguing – only presentation, testimony, and prayers among an atmoshpere of love, acceptance, harmony, peace, and sharing. No person or group dominates another. Individuals may continue in their own formal church or religion.

†*We are of God: he that knoweth God heareth us; he that is not of God, heareth not us. Hereby know we the Spirit of Truth, and the spirit of error.* (1 John 4:6) This scripture refers to Christ's Apostles and Disciples, i.e. the New Testament.

Chapter 2
Failure of Reason

With the development of the electron microscope and the advancement of the physical sciences leading to the discovery of molecular composition, we find that there is more space than 'solid' in a table top. Dr. Einstein, in his theory of relativity, posits that mass is simply concentrated energy. In light of this, think about what St. Paul said almost 2000 years ago, *"Through faith we understand that the worlds were framed by the Word of God, so that things which are seen were not made of things which do appear."* (Hebrews 11:3) People who rationalize life and the world to the "n'th" degree may 'think' that with evolution they can explain away creation and the need for, or the existence of, God. Probably the same type of assumptions could 'explain away' evil, with psychological concepts such as the 'unconscious' (or subconscious), and thus dismiss Satan as myth. These 'thinkers' are deluding themselves as much as were the subjects of that kingdom whose king went out among his subjects in his 'birthday suit' and all the people were praising him on how beautiful his new suit was, until a little boy said, 'But the king is naked!' People can be concerned with appearances and being politically correct to the extent of deceiving themselves and living a lie.

Darwinian Evolution does not replace the necessity of God, nor does the Freudian concept of the 'unconscious' (subconscious) replace the existence of Satan. Clinical psychologists can 'explain' why some people act the way they do (afraid to love or be loved, or always angry or paranoid, etc.), but they cannot account for the other people that were brought up in similar ways, or even in the same family, who do not behave in those same pathological ways. Furthermore, sometimes, no matter how logical the psychologist's explanation, no matter how much it may appear to tie all the loose ends together and 'explain' the psychopathology, it does not change the person's pathological behaviors, and often, even with highly motivated effort, the person himself can but make small changes toward healthier and happier interactions with other people. Psychotherapy can be helpful, but it is not the entire answer and often is helpless to change a person's aberrant behavior. Jesus said, ". . . *Verily I say unto you, Except ye be converted, and become as little children, ye shall not enter into the kingdom of heaven.*" (Matthew 18:3) "*Beware lest any man spoil you through philosophy and vain deceit, after the tradition of men, after the rudiments of the world, and not after Christ.*" (Colossians 2:8) "*Howbeit when He, the Spirit of truth, is come, He will guide you into all truth: for He shall not speak of Himself; but whatsoever He shall hear, that shall He speak; and He will shew you things to come.*" (John 16:13)

Pride and ego may build nations, but they destroy people. Pride, ego and deceit may achieve material ends, but they corrupt in the process. Natural man is a predatory animal, each one of whom, in one way or another, wants to be the king of beasts. A natural, carnal man can be bestial, in the worst sense of the word. Natural man and spiritual man are not citizens of the same world. The transition from a natural man to a spiritual man cannot be a continuum because it involves a hiatus, a leap of faith in Jesus Christ, and the end of the natural or carnal or physical man is death, whereas the destiny of the spiritual man is immortality. Evil does exist, but it will not always be; good also exists and always will. Someone said that 'evil has within it the seeds of its own destruction'.

Human achievements, the great monuments of civilization, are all mixed blessings. Science is not God and science cannot take the place of God; it is entirely neutral toward and ignorant of the individual. "*Oh Timothy keep that which is committed to thy trust, avoiding vain babblings, and oppositions of science falsely so called.*" (1 Timothy 6:20) As corporate capitalism grows larger and larger, it has a tendency to sacrifice the family life upon the altar of commercialism, uprooting families, sending them to places hundreds of miles from the parent's childhood homes and consigning the children to new schools, new classmates, new neighbors. Demanding of executives their total allegiance and becoming the number one priority of their time, the family comes in a distant second. Furthermore, as government also grows larger, it becomes more and more bureaucratic and progressively pushes aside the individual and the reality of freedom, as well.

Within a period of sixty-five years, the United States of America has fallen from a prosperous nation of free people who were responsible not only for themselves but for others, in a common sense and compassionate way. Through the occurrence of a great emergency, the Great Depression of the thirties, certain vital principles were set aside because, by then, the Age of the Robber Barons had been in full bloom for over a half of a century and greed and materialism, among the populace, were beginning to replace the deep religious convictions set forth by our Founding Fathers – which, by the way, reflected the populace at that time as well. So America elected and reelected and reelected and reelected its first 'king', Franklin Roosevelt. Quoting the prophet Samuel, it is becoming easier to relate to the following text. *"And said unto him, Behold, thou art old, and thy sons walk not in thy ways: now make us a king to judge us like all nations. But the thing displeased Samuel, when they said, Give us a king to judge us.*

"And Samuel prayed unto the Lord, and the Lord said unto Samuel, ***Hearken unto the voice of the people in all that they say unto thee: for they have not rejected thee, but they have rejected Me, that I should not reign over them. According to all the works which they have done since the day that I brought them up out of Egypt even unto this day, wherewith they have forsaken Me, and served other gods, so do they also unto thee. Now therefore hearken unto their voice: howbeit yet protest solemnly unto them, and show them the manner of the king that shall reign over them.*** *And Samuel told all the words of the Lord unto the people that asked of him a king. And he said, This will be the manner of the king that shall reign over you: He will take your sons, and appoint them for himself, for his chariots, and to be his horsemen; and some shall run before his chariots. And he will appoint him captains over thousands, and captains over fifties; and will set them to*

ear his ground, and to reap his harvest, and to make his instruments of war, and instruments of his chariots. And he will take your daughters to be confectionaries, and to be cooks, and to be bakers.

"And he will take your fields, and your vineyards, and your oliveyards, even the best of them, and give them to his servants. And he will take the tenth of your seed, and of your vineyards , and give to his officers, and to his servants. And he will take your menservants, and your maidservants, and your goodliest young men, and your asses, and put them to his work. He will take the tenth of your sheep: and ye shall be his servants. And ye shall cry out in that day because of your king which ye shall have chosen you; and the Lord will not hear you in that day." (1 Samuel 8:5-18) Today, the government (Federal, State and Local, including both income and sales taxes) extracts over 40% of our earnings!

To quote briefly from a very prophetic book, *The Road to Serfdom*[7] by a brilliant economist that was printed fifty years ago and, because of its even increased relevancy to our times, has recently been re-published on its fiftieth anniversary: "It is the price of democracy that the possibilities of conscious control are restricted to the fields where true agreement exists and that in some fields things must be left to chance . . . Democratic government has worked successfully where, and so long as, the functions of government were, by a widely accepted creed, restricted to fields where agreement among a majority could be achieved by free discussion; It is now often said that democracy will not tolerate 'capitalism'. If 'capitalism' means here a competitive system based on free disposal over private property, it is far more important to realize that only within this system is democracy possible. When it becomes dominated by collectivist creed, democracy will inevitably destroy itself."[7](Pages 77-78) Even democracy is but a faint shadow of Christianity. And another excellent author has recently written a book that should be on everyone's reading list that is concerned with the decline of our society in this age of promiscuity, violence and depravity. From, *The Theme is Freedom*, by Stanton Evans,

"Nowhere is THE CULTURAL CONFLICT of the modern era more apparent than in dispute about the place of religion in the civic order. Here the battle is overt, relentless, and pervasive – with traditional belief and custom retreating before a secularist onslaught in our courts and other public institutions."[3](Page 270)

Hope plays such an important part in the 'journey' of faith, it seems that there is, at times, almost a continuous battle to hold on to faith and that, without hope, it would be a losing fight. This, however, is what faith is all about. By definition, faith cannot be proven. It is as St. Paul states, "*Now faith is the substance of things hoped for, the evidence of things unseen.*" (Hebrews 11:1) Furthermore, it is worth the effort, "*But without faith it is impossible to please Him: for he that cometh to God must believe that He is, and that He is a rewarder of them that diligently seek Him.*" (Hebrews 11:6) We need to understand this as a spiritual battle against our carnal (physical – sensual) nature and against the forces of evil (garnered and directed by Satan). Being on a spiritual plane, it is most important that we seek God's will and look at our time here on earth as a sojourn, an odyssey; we are, so to speak, aliens from another world. We are aliens in the sense that we are alive on a doomed planet (earth), in a natural body (physical), and cursed with a carnal mind (sensual), **but** have chosen to, and are in the process of, becoming spiritually minded through Jesus Christ and the Holy Spirit.

Thus, we are aliens from those who have not made this choice and are indeed citizens of this evil empire (the world) whose ruler is the 'prince of air' (Satan) and who are thus headed for death. As aliens, we are headed toward immortality in a new world, a new body and a life of **being** in the presence of God forever. The joy, peace, perfection and love in that life to come are ineffable – beyond our ability to comprehend or describe. Of course, we need to obtain the necessities of physical life, but beyond that, we are to pursue spiritual gifts and to try to live on a spiritual plane as much as we can. That would mean that love, for example, toward God and man, forms the basis of our actions and thoughts. "*And now* *abideth faith, hope, charity (love), these three; but the greatest of these is charity (love).*" (1 Corinthians 13:13) Please notice that hope is one of the two qualities singled out as ranking next to love. Thus, it is very important not to be discouraged when it seems we don't have evidence of God's presence in our lives; the struggle for faith vitally and inevitably involves hope.

A new, young or growing Christian often feels lost and doesn't sense the presence of God and at times, interprets this as either not having faith or as being rejected by God. Nothing could be further from the truth. In fact, all this doubt is the very action of Satan; he hates humans and wants to keep them separated from God to break down their faith. Think of your position as similar to when you were a child at your first day of school (kindergarten) and you are lost, at sea, frightened, feeling inadequate and alone. Where are your 'all-powerful' parents who can fix anything, can solve all your new problems? They are not with you, they could be but they are not; you have to fend for yourself and learn to defend yourself (against bullies), learn how to socialize and make friends. (Or if you are a parent, you know how hard it was to thrust your child out into the world alone without your presence to protect him or her from hurt or harm, but you knew that to insert yourself in your child's new life would have been disastrous for his or her future peer relationships.) It is helpful for a struggling Christian to realize that for reasons he or she does not comprehend, God is always with you, but your faith is constantly tried and hope must be ever present. (Please read Romans 12:2, on how you gradually come to know God's will.)

We must want to believe in Jesus Christ and continue to try to grow and understand and practice what the New Testament presents. Human reason is just a system of thought, as is logic, Newtonian physics, Euclidian geometry and Einsteinian relativity, just to cite a few examples. However, God is not restricted to human systems of thought or even to the process of thought. Faith transcends logic; it is outside of logic. God can be postulated and conceptualized by existences and happenings, but He cannot be proven to be, just as faith cannot be 'proven'; in fact, to 'prove' faith would be an oxymoron. Great systems of thought, such as Darwinian evolution and Freudian psychology, come to be commonly accepted as not just theories but factual sciences! In reality, evolution and psychology have become panchrestons (a broadly inclusive thesis that is intended to cover all possible variations within an area of concern and that, in practice, usually proves to be an unacceptable oversimplification). Despite Darwin and Freud, God cannot be invalidated, and by God I refer to the Christian God of the New Testament.

The revelation wherein God gave the ten commandments to Moses reveals that man was not inherently good, he might have been neither good nor bad, but he was not, by nature, good. This had been made clear in the Garden of Eden when God told man not to eat of the tree of knowledge of good and evil. In fact, that was God's first commandment to man, showing that man did not know the difference between good and evil – and so was without the ability to sin and was, therefore, 'sinless'. Yet the ability to sin was in him in the sense that he disobeyed God's only rule or law shortly after it was pronounced! So, as St. Paul says, the law was good and must be fulfilled because evil does and did exist from the beginning of our world.

Even our courts say that ignorance of the law does not excuse the offender. So God was loving when He laid down the law. It was not only to protect the society of man, but also to reveal the presence of sin in the world (Satan apparently already existed before man was placed on earth) and the purpose of the law was to reveal the presence of sin, its nature and our susceptibility to it. (Chapter 7 in Romans enlarges on this.) Otherwise, man could never have become spiritually hungry and sought to be 'good'. More importantly, the law created the possibility of man becoming not only obedient to God, but willingly so. This does establish that the world has been susceptible to sin from the beginning, why we do not know.

Furthermore, evil has its promoters and there are references to Satan in many places in both the Old and New Testaments (see e.g., 1 Chronicles 21:1[Old Testament] and Revelations 12:9 [New Testament]). Actually, Satan has 19 references in the Old Testament and 35 in the New and there are 60 references to the devil in the New Testament, none in the Old (there are 4 references to devils in the Old Testament and 51 in the new); evil has innumerable references in both Old and New Testaments, (400-500). However, the original creation was good including man (in essence). And it is that perfect essence, the spiritual man that we aspire to in the coming life, and that is determined by whether we choose good or evil, spiritual thinking and being or carnal thinking and being. The important point is that to choose the good can only come about through Jesus Christ crucified and risen again, and the Holy Spirit being allowed to work within us because of God's grace (". . .the Divine influence upon the heart, and its reflection in the life. . . " [Strong's concordance1955-charis])[14]. In other words, we were created with **freedom to choose** and the purpose of our life is to exercise this freedom and, most importantly, to each of us – to make the 'right' choice: spirituality through Jesus Christ.

We cannot seem to grasp what St. John says so eloquently, *"In the beginning was the Word, and the Word was with God, and the Word was God. The same was in the beginning with God. All things were made by Him; and without Him was not anything made that was made. In Him was life; and the life was the light of men. And the light shineth in darkness; and the darkness comprehended it not. There was a man sent from God, whose name was John. The same came for a witness, to bear witness of the Light, that all men through Him might believe. He was not that Light, but was sent to bear witness of that Light. That was the true Light, which lighteth every man that cometh into the world. He was in the world, and the world was made by Him, and the world knew Him not. He came unto His own, and His own received Him not. But as many as received Him, to them gave He power to become the sons of God, even to them that believe on His name: Which were born, not of blood, nor of the will of the flesh, nor of the will of man, but of*

God. And the Word was made flesh, and dwelt among us, (and we beheld His glory, the glory as of the only begotten of the Father) full of grace and truth. John bare witness of Him, and cried, saying, This was He of Whom I spoke, He that cometh after me is preferred before me; for He was before me. And of His fulness have all we received, and grace for grace. For the law was given by Moses, but grace and truth came by Jesus Christ." (John 1:1-17)

Hope must abide if faith is to endure. "*These all died in faith, not having received the promises, but having seen them afar off, and were persuaded of them, and embraced them, and confessed that they were strangers and pilgrims on the earth."* (Hebrews 11:13) And faith must be present if our minds are to be open. "*For unto us was the gospel preached, as well as unto them: but the word preached did not profit them, not being mixed with faith in them that heard it."* (Hebrews 4:2) Moreover, each of us, holding on to hope and growing in faith, will have a relationship with God. *"For this is the covenant that I will make with the house of Israel after those days, saith the Lord; I will put My laws into their mind, and write them in their hearts: and I will be to them a God, and they shall be to Me a people: And they shall not teach every man his neighbour, and every man his brother, saying, Know the Lord: for all shall know Me, from the least to the greatest."* (Hebrews 8:10-11) "*For there is no difference between the Jew and the Greek: for the same Lord over all is rich unto all that call upon Him."* (Romans 10:12)

As pointed out elsewhere, one of the basic statements of the New Testament, in my opinion is, "*And now abideth faith, hope, charity, these three; but the greatest of these is charity."* (1 Corinthians 13:13) (Charity meaning love.) Now faith is a gift to us from God, "*For by grace are ye saved through faith; and that not of yourselves: it is the gift of God."* (Ephesians 2:8) Hope sustains faith, "*Now faith is the substance of things hoped for, the evidence of things not seen."* (Hebrews 11:1), and hope then becomes the substance of faith. Faith is so basic, it leads the author of

Hebrews to say, "*But without faith it is impossible to please Him: for He that cometh to God must believe that He is, and that He is a rewarder of them that diligently seek Him.*" (Hebrews 11:6) Further, we must demonstrate our faith, but in order to do that, we must know what our faith is. First, it is that God exists and second, that He loves us so much that He entered our reality (the world). Our world has become a VIRTUAL REALITY, i.e. artificial reality because of our focus on ourselves. He showed us what we are, **spiritual**, and how we are to enter into **ACTUAL REALITY** through the 'way', the 'truth' and the 'life' of Jesus Christ.

In other words, God became a part of His own creation for a while (in the form of Jesus Christ) in order to rescue us from mortality and judgment. He is still with us in the form of the Holy Spirit (Holy Ghost or Comforter). It is natural to have a struggle with faith as Satan opposes it at every step of the way and God tells us that we may have to suffer in the body as Christ suffered, which goes against what many would like to believe. However, when we have faith, we are blessed with the Spiritual fruits such as peace, joy and love; no matter what our bodies are enduring. It seems at times that the best humans – most admirable, moral and 'good', are the very ones that have the most grievous falls into sin and perhaps two suppositions could help make some sense of this. First, they would be the ones that Satan would want to destroy (the book of Job cites a good example); and second, this may be the only way some of them can be convinced of the existence of evil and of the need for judgment to occur, i.e., for them to realize that human nature is not inherently good just because they themselves tend to be honest, upright and loving. Furthermore, that they are not perfect either and they, along with everyone else, need Christ and that Christ had to die for our salvation as a propitiation of our sins and sinful nature.

As a matter of fact, there are so many antinomies (a contradiction between two philosophical principles, each of which is taken to be true or between inferences correctly drawn from such principles; also a conflict or opposition between the products of reason and experience) and paradoxes (a statement or sentiment that is seemingly contradictory or opposed to common sense and yet, perhaps, is true in fact) that arise in human experience and thought, that it is easy to convince ourselves, or to be convinced of what we want to believe. "*And be not conformed to this world: but be ye transformed by the renewing of your mind, that ye may prove what is that good, and acceptable, and perfect, will of God.*" (Romans 12:2) "*But let every man prove his own work, and then shall he have rejoicing in himself alone, and not in another.*" (Galatians 6:4) "*Prove all things; hold fast that which is good.*" (1 Thessalonians 5:21)

Chapter 3
Deceit of Wisdom

The marvels of man that reveal the 'wonder' of the human brain is more and more attributed to the 'unlimited' ability of the human race in general, or to the genius of some individual in particular, rather than to God revealing these things to us through inspiration. He has created the human brain capable of these things in the first place. However He did it, He is the original, ultimate and only source of all essences and existences (living and inanimate). Men do build wonderful things, but they are but dim reflections of what God has in store for those who give Him recognition, obedience, worship and honor. *"For Christ sent me not to baptize, but to preach the gospel, not with wisdom of words, lest the cross of Christ should be made of none effect. For the preaching of the cross is to them that perish foolishness; but unto us which are saved it is the power of God. For it is written, I will destroy the wisdom of the wise, and will bring to nothing the understanding of the prudent. Where is the wise? where is the scribe? where is the disputer of this world? hath not God made foolish the wisdom of this world? For after that in the wisdom of God the world by wisdom knew not God, it pleased God by the foolishness of preaching to save them that believe."* (1 Corinthians 1:17-21)

The human journey through life without a living faith in God through Jesus Christ and the Holy Spirit is not fulfilling and is without true purpose and meaning. For example, does it really mean that having a billion dollars or making 500 million dollars in one year will make anyone really happy? How effective is any other 'faith' in helping anyone from being trapped by drugs or in overcoming paranoia? In fact, it may contribute to both these afflictions. Can a humanly devised substitute philosophy or 'faith' help a person deal with imprisonment and injustice or cope with cancer or AIDS? When these types of things happen to people, it humbles some and they seek and find God (who is always waiting ready to encompass them with forgiveness and love through His Son, Jesus Christ). A child of God, that is, anyone who accepts Christ and turns from unbelief or disbelief to faith in Him and His life, may have afflictions, but no matter what their state of being, there is a bedrock of peace, love and hope. Money and power cannot buy this and, sadly, they get in the way of it, making it harder to become as a child toward God. *"And we know that all things work together for good to them that love God, to them who are the called according to His purpose."* (Romans 8:28)

It is interesting to note that *nowhere* in the King James New Testament does the word **'justice'** appear! It does appear in the Old Testament from Genesis to Ezekiel. However, the word **'judgment'** does appear in the New Testament over 75 times, in various forms and usages, and in the Old Testament, well over two hundred times. Since Christ or the Messiah has come to earth in the form of Jesus of Nazareth, justice has been served as He shed His blood for us to redeem us from our sins. In other words, JUSTICE HAS BEEN DONE – NOW ONLY JUDGMENT REMAINS. So, we either accept Jesus as Christ and follow His way and His truth along with the subtle guidance of the Holy Spirit to become spiritually minded and immortal, *or* we continue to worship man, science, physical nature, and/or sensuous hedonism, leading to physical and spiritual death – whatever that entails. The New Testament has promises that are given to us in the here and now for our strength, hope, faith and ability to love. For example, a few such passages: *"And ye shall know the truth, and the truth shall make you free."* (John 8:32); *"For now we see through a glass, darkly; but then face to face: now I know in part; but then shall I know even as also I am known."* (1 Corinthians 13:12); *"And the peace of God, which passeth all understanding, shall keep your hearts and minds through Christ Jesus."* (Phillipians 4:7); *"There is no fear in love; but perfect love casteth out fear: because fear hath torment. He that feareth is not made perfect in love."* (1 John 4:18)

It is interesting and of significant consequence to note that, on the other hand, the word **faith** appears only two times in the

Old Testament, but it appears over 200 times in the New Testament. It seems clear that before Christ the emphasis was on justice and judgment, but that since Christ we are in an era emphasizing faith.

We are free to live independently of God here in this physical existence if we so choose not to live by His grace; however, the end of that is death – finality. On the other hand, we are free to choose to seek and find God and to determine His will for us and to begin our immortal journey of spiritual being, which is an immortal existence of the essence that He created as man. If this is our free choice, then eventually we must 'find' Christ for *"Jesus saith unto him, I am the way, the truth, and the life: no man cometh unto the Father, but by Me."* (John 14:6) Furthermore, *"But the Comforter, which is the Holy Ghost, Whom the Father will send in My name, He shall teach you all things, and bring all things to your remembrance, whatsoever I have said unto you."* (John 14:26) The spiritual is reality, whereas the physical is temporal, and is that temporary state wherein God's creation, man, has complete freedom of choice. If you choose to be independent of God, making the physical, the sensual and the material, the be all and end all of your life – then you are without God in the world, and with that choice, the 'god' of this world (yourself, another human, a human creation or the devil) takes over and you are at the mercy of the vagaries of this physical world without recourse to help from God; *unless* and until you see the futility and emptiness of life without God *and begin* to seek Him, *"For they that are after the flesh do mind the things of the flesh; but they that are after the Spirit the things of the Spirit. For to be carnally minded is death; but to be spiritually minded is life and peace. Because the carnal mind is enmity against God: for it is not subject to the law of God, neither indeed can be."* (Romans 8:5-7)

Distill the words of Jesus Christ and ponder what kind of a world we all would have if they represented our creed. *"Jesus said unto him, Thou shalt love the Lord thy God with all thy heart, and with all thy soul, and with all thy mind. This is the first and great commandment. And the second is like unto it, Thou shalt love thy neighbour as thyself. On these two commandments hang all the law and the prophets."* (Matthew 22:37-40) Ask yourself how that creed could be bettered. There is no philosophy nor psychology nor science nor any religious leader that has ever presented a better creed.

Then realize it will never happen in this physical world. For one thing, there is no way to rid the world of greed, self-seeking, lust, violence and perversion, not to mention natural disasters, famines and pestilences. This is a physical, deteriorating world and it is inhabited by flawed human beings. *"Hereafter I will not talk much with you: for the prince of this world cometh, and hath nothing in Me."* (John 14:30) *"Be sober, be vigilant: because your adversary the devil, as a roaring lion, walketh about, seeking whom he may devour: Whom resist stedfast in the faith, knowing that the same afflictions are accomplished in your brethren that are in the world."* (1 Peter 5:8-9)

I believe only those relatively few humans (few, relative to the billions who have lived) who seek God through Jesus Christ and the New Testament with prayerful guidance from the Holy Spirit have an opportunity to inherit a spiritual kingdom and an immortal life that will far surpass any possible physical world or life that man can imagine, or even dream.

Others never exposed to Christ may be inheritors as well. *"For not the hearers of the law are just before God, but the doers of the law shall be justified. For when the Gentiles, which have not the law, do by nature the things contained in the law, these, having not the law, are a law unto themselves: Which show the work of the law written in their hearts, their conscience also bearing witness, and their thoughts the mean while accusing or else excusing one another."* (Romans 2:13-15) **BUT**, if you know of Jesus Christ and if you have read the New Testament or heard it preached, you are without excuse and in real danger of the 'lake of fire' **IF** you are not *trying* to reject your carnal mind and *seeking* to understand what Christ accomplished; allowing the love of God into your heart. (See page 204)

Christ was kind and He was crucified. Christ was loving and He was crucified. Christ obeyed the civil authorities and their laws and yet He was crucified. Why? Because men are evil and reject the truth; they are self-seeking, want control of others, possession of things and power. Present day America has become a 'victim-oriented' society wherein the perpetrator 'becomes' the 'victim'. *"But evil men and seducers shall wax worse and worse, deceiving, and being deceived."* (2 Timothy 3:13) *"But the tongue can no man tame; it is an unruly evil, full of deadly poison."* (James 3:8)

Once again, hear the beauty and the simplicity of language from an inspired St. John, allowing its eternal truth to be absorbed into your inner being. *"That which was from the beginning, which we have heard, which we have seen with our eyes, which we have looked upon, and our hands have handled, of the Word of life; (For the life was manifested, and we have seen it, and bear witness, and show unto you that eternal life, which was with the Father, and was manifested unto us;) That which we have seen and heard declare we unto you, that ye also may have fellowship with us: and truly our fellowship is with the Father, and with His Son Jesus Christ. And these things write we unto you, that your joy may be full. This then is the message which we have heard of Him, and declare unto you, that God is light, and in Him is no darkness at all. If we say that we have fellowship with Him, and walk in darkness, we lie, and do not the truth: But if we walk in the light, as He is in the light, we have fellowship one with another, and the blood of Jesus Christ His Son cleanseth us from all sin. If we say that we have no sin, we deceive ourselves, and the truth is not in us. If we confess our sins, He is faithful and just to forgive us our sins, and to cleanse us from all unrighteousness. If we say that we have not sinned, we make Him a liar, and His word is not in us."* (1 John 1:1-10)

One needs to always attempt to maintain a sense of 'community' even if it is, of necessity, restricted to long-distance communication – in which event one must still attempt to love one's physical neighbors. Perhaps the hardest 'cross' to bear is to love your neighbor as yourself; I take that to mean loving all men. A thought I keep in mind is that no matter how bad or evil some men are, it is conceivable that I could be just as evil or even worse, with the 'right' circumstances starting from my birth. I speculate that if from infancy I had been born into fame, power, wealth or adoration and all those around me were at my beck and call, I might have gotten out of touch with reality and even believed that I was 'god-like' and could do no wrong, that I was a law unto myself! On the other hand, suppose I was born into abject poverty AND cruelty or neglect; what kind of a creature might I have become? It could be very illuminating to give the potential some real thought. There are so many combinations of life circumstances and experiences, the possibilities are endless as to what one would be capable of becoming – in an evil way. Even with this knowledge in the intellect, it is still virtually impossible to 'feel' what that means, and so it is extremely difficult to identify with a wife beater, a junkie or a slum landlord, for example. But love is empathy, invoking forgiveness when it is asked for, with repentance present.

However, as my quote from Oswald Chambers[1] pointed out in Chapter One, Jesus came to not only cleanse sinners from their sin (a different emphasis than 'forgiving'), but to change us and to obliterate sin. Although that perfection may be impossible in our earthly existence, we can approach it and, I believe, Christ's sacrifice washes the remainder away. That was why Christ had to die for our sins, and did not come just to 'forgive' our sins. In baseball analogy, it would be similar to a bunt whereby the bunter is called out but a runner scores. In other words, Christ sacrificed His life for ours.

Stop to consider the 'heroes' in the Bible; Moses disobeyed God and wasn't allowed into the promised land; Jacob could at times appear to be a mean and petty man and he received return in kind; David committed a terrible crime with Bathsheba – and paid a price. And so it was that God used humans and all humans are flawed, but He uses us and 'forgives' us and loves us. It helps speak for the authenticity of the Bible in that it does not 'whitewash' its 'great' men. So if these giants of the Bible had so many 'warts', isn't it plausible to think: 1) that He can and does love us and long for our allowing Him into our life; and 2) that we should try a little harder to love all men. We are all brothers and we ARE all sinners – needing Christ and forgiveness – no matter how 'clean' we think our lives are, no matter how self-righteous we feel.

In fact, our distance from Him is probably in direct proportion to how self-righteous we feel about ourselves. *"The heart is deceitful above all things, and desperately wicked: who can know it?"* (Jeremiah 17:9). But take heart, *"And He said unto me, My grace is sufficient for thee: for My strength is made perfect in weakness. Most gladly therefore will I rather glory in my infirmities, that the power of Christ may rest upon me."* (2 Corinthians 12:9). *"I can do all things through Christ which strengtheneth me."* (Philemon 4:13)

As David said, *"Blessed is he whose transgression is forgiven, whose sin is covered. Blessed is the man unto whom the Lord imputeth not iniquity and in whose spirit there is no guile."* (Psalm 32:1-2). Saint Paul reiterates this: *"Saying, Blessed are they whose iniquities are forgiven, and whose sins are covered. Blessed is the man to whom the Lord will not impute sin."* (Romans 4:7-8). (Guile meaning: remissness, treachery, deceit, falseness, idle, slack or slothful.) David, as you recall, (2 Samuel 11:2-17) committed a horrible sin and yet it was 'put away' by God. Saul persecuted, terribly, the new Christian sect until, on the road to Damascus, he was struck down and blinded by God, Who asked him, *"...Saul, Saul, why persecutest thou Me?"* (Acts 9:4). God restored his sight, enlightened him and, from thenceforth, he was renamed Paul and he accomplished great work from then on in the Christian cause.

To me, this shows that if you are honest with yourself and seeking God's will, even when you are wrong (honestly mistaken), if you are living in faith and working toward a thorough-going faith, God will forgive you, correct you and bless you. Further to the point; *"Hast thou faith? have it to thyself before God. Happy is he that condemneth not himself in that thing which he alloweth.*

And he that doubteth is damned if he eat, because he eateth not of faith: for whatsoever is not of faith is sin." (Romans 14:22-23) It also indicates to me that one can sin grievously and 'knowingly' (i.e., temporarily denies or 'sets aside' one's belief system or rationalizes) and still be forgiven by God if one is truly contrite and throws himself or herself upon God's love and mercy and Christ's atonement.

Chapter 4
Illusion of Perception

Man is ultimately either a spiritual being or a carnal being, and the latter includes natural man, physical man, material man and sensual (or sensuous) man. All but the spiritual man are products of their senses and are locked into the physical world, and have thus corrupted their minds. Logically, at least, the mind is the residing place of the spirit, but because of the condition into which humans are born (namely, separation from God) they have enthroned their perception as paramount. We utilize logic to establish 'control' over our environment and emotions, elevating 'feelings' (both physical and mental) as the ultimate 'good'. Unfortunately, these types of feelings die with the physical death (annihilation of the brain). From birth to death, some humans appear to be predominantly carnal; however, most humans are a combination of spirituality and carnality. It is this very struggle, and **only this struggle** between being spiritual and being carnal and its outcome, which decides the final destiny of each and every human. <u>Nothing else is of permanent consequence.</u>

However, there is no death for the spiritual being, and the only way to spirituality is through Jesus Christ. True life and living, whether 'in' the physical body or in the spirit, is having the presence of God, or His Holy Spirit. *"But the fruit of the Spirit is love, joy, peace, longsuffering, gentleness, goodness, faith, meekness, temperance: against such there is no law. And they that are Christ's have crucified the flesh with the affections and lusts. If we live in the Spirit, let us also walk in the Spirit."* (Galatians 5:22-25)

All lust, greed, violence, possessiveness, envy, hate and strife come from a consuming physical desire, which can be created by the interpretation of what we see, feel, smell, touch, hear or taste. This interpretation is called perception. For example, if you like cars, their appearance (curves & contours), their feel to your touch (smoothness, sleekness), the way the motor sounds (purrs or roars), the smell of the newness inside or the faint tinge of oil and gas around the engine, and even the 'taste' – figuratively (a Corvette is preferred over a Porsche – it is just a matter of 'taste'). If this generates a consuming passion for cars, i.e., if these perceptions create an obsession for the feel of power or speed or a sense of superiority, it then becomes lustful and a source of pride. Your perception of the desired object (be it money, land, power, sex, cars or whatever) is all in your mind. Even sex is in the mind; the ejaculation is physical, but the orgasm is mental. It is upon these perceptions that one's self-image (ego) is based.

The journey of the self through life is to replace the carnal mind with the spiritual mind, and in so doing replacing self with God. The natural identity acquired through our experiences, learning and feedback from 'important others' (parents, siblings, relatives, teachers, peers and heroes) is in fact, our carnal mind. This change from the carnal mind to the spiritual mind is achieved through denying ourselves, belief in Jesus Christ and following the guidance of the Holy Spirit. Denying one's self is putting God at one's center and then, other people first in one's life.

If you are a parent, perhaps you have had your own child misbehave or displease you so that you expressed your displeasure with him? What did it take for you to forgive him, or to even forget about the misbehavior? What did you feel when your child came to you and asked if you still loved him, or even simply said, 'I'm sorry'? In this light, imagine how God would be willing to accept, love and bless any human who asked forgiveness and came to Him, even though He is perfect and we are not. Through Christ He would, because then He sees us newly born in Christ who has cleansed us and separated us from all our imperfections, mistakes, disobedience and even wickedness. (See Paul in Romans 7:14-21, or refer back to page 19.)

Once you begin to believe this and keep seeking Him, He will open up your understanding and awareness of Him and His love, more and more. If you can forgive your child and love that child even if he is bad, God's love and forgiveness is certainly able to do that much and more! He does love and accept you and He has been able to reconcile His perfection (including His justice) with you and your imperfections through Jesus Christ upon Whom has been rendered the judgment due you and so now you are free from judgment – as long as you begin to walk 'in the Spirit' and keep trying, no matter if you keep disappointing yourself. Just know, He is always loving you and helping you to "walk the walk" and furthermore, your heart will begin to open more and soften, and you will realize you are in God's care and begin to experience His peace, love and presence more and more (I believe the degree and frequency depends on your efforts and your needs and God's grace).

"But when that which is perfect is come, then that which is in part shall be done away. When I was a child, I spake as a child, I understood as a child, I thought as a child: but when I became a man, I put away childish things. For now we see through a glass, darkly; but then face to face: now I know in part; but then shall I know even as also I am known." (1 Corinthians 13:10-12)

One of the major problems in American society today is the lack of personal initiative and assuming responsibility for one's own behavior. Some people are drawn to hypnosis because they want someone else to 'change' them or make their lives better. This stems from a detachment from God, that is to say, not having Him as one's constant counselor. Instead, God is mostly a symbol to turn to only in the direst need and then half-heartedly because there is such a shallow layer of faith, just a surface veneer, if any, in many individual's and family's lives today. However, God is not a symbol; He is not only alive, He is life. And if we do not 'know' Him, it is absolutely essential, vital, that we allow Him to make Himself known to us. *"Jesus answered and said unto him, If a man love Me, he will keep My words: and My Father will love him, and We will come unto him, and make Our abode with him."* (John 14:23) If we don't 'know' God, we don't know life, we only know virtuality. *"And when He was demanded of the Pharisees, when the kingdom of God should come, He answered them and said, The kingdom of God cometh not with observation: Neither shall they say, Lo here! or, lo there! for, behold, the kingdom of God is within you."* (Luke 17:20-21)

Concomitant with this is an increasing reliance on the State, which increasingly takes away the person's freedom and money. This represents a backward trend from Christianity, which really introduced personal freedom and human rights into organized society. Referring to Evans[3] in his book *The Theme is Freedom*, "The classical way of thinking led inexorably to untrammeled power in the state, and to subjugation of the individual. The biblical model leads to limitations on that power, and hence to freedom." (p. 135) An increasing number of authors are echoing these sentiments. We are desperate as a society to stop the political abuse of power and the rampage of crime.

Today's politicians tout individual's 'rights' as the route to greater freedom, whereas in fact, it is the road to slavery and 'serfdom' and a corruption of human rights (which are broader and more inclusive than individual rights that tend to cancel each other out and leave the bureaucracy in more absolute control). The following from Hayek[7] *The Road to Serfdom*, "It is well known that particularly the scientists and engineers, who had so loudly claimed to be the leaders on the march to a new and better world, submitted more readily than almost any other class to the new tyranny." (p. 209) This was referring to Nazi Germany. "Apart from the intellectual influences which we have illustrated by two instances, the impetus of the movement toward totalitarianism comes mainly from the two great vested interests: organized capital and organized labor." (p. 213) Our founding fathers sought Divine guidance but they also approached their task with 1) the venality of mankind in mind, and 2) that seats of power have a tendency to be self-serving. They thus sought to counteract this with balances of power. However, it is when collusion enters in that opposing powerful interests decide to combine in order to dominate and manipulate the populace. What they did not foresee was the tremendous growth and influence of capitalistic corporations and monopolies, nor did they see the scientific advances ahead. We must, therefore, make strong readjustments and, without our having some 'absolutes' and goals, we will lose out to unscrupulous leaders. We must believe that there is purpose to existence and that God is at the center.

"While they promise them liberty, they themselves are the servants of corruption: for of whom a man is overcome, of the same is he brought in bondage." (2 Peter 2:19) We will not take to heart the message of Christ that we must have an everyday living faith in God, the 'sine qua non' of putting into practice love toward our fellow human beings. It really is quite simple but impossible without a nation exercising everyday reliance on God. There is no other answer and, until pride and greed are pushed aside by love and faith, we are headed toward catastrophe.

Quoting from Howard[8] in *The Death of Common Sense*, ". . . Until the last few decades, however, rights were not something to shout about. They were the bedrock of our society, something we would give our lives to defend, but not something people thought much about as they made it through each day. Rights were synonymous with freedom, protection against being ordered around by government or others." (p. 116)

He had described a sidewalk toilet, which had been perfected, that was a boon for New Yorkers, until the Mayor's Office of the Disabled using New York's antidiscrimination law had them banned because they couldn't accommodate wheelchairs. So no one had toilets available on the streets of New York. Instead, anyone shopping or sightseeing or even on the way to an engagement, walking on the street, had to find a subway entrance and go down into the subway to find a toilet. He gives many examples of 'special rights' and how irrationally and unreasonably they have affected the rights of the rest of us.

One of the things a clinical psychologist is taught in graduate school to be on guard against, while giving an I.Q. test for intelligence, is being swayed unconsciously by looks or personality. It is too easy to unknowingly 'help' the person or to give the person extra credit on an answer when he or she is attractive or personable, and this applies to psychiatric evaluations and other kinds of psychological testing as well. This type of training is needed because often this bias enters in unconsciously, and therefore, the examiner must be alert to this ever present 'danger'.

Politicians make regular use of this human tendency, and so it is becoming more and more the case that crafty, deceitful politicians get elected because of their looks and charm, not because of their character or performance. Despotic governments and cancerous bureaucracies often are elected democratically because people believe their words, which are either outright lies or consist of a language of perverted meanings given to otherwise sound and good concepts. More and more decisions are made by committees or behind the scenes because no one wants to stand and be counted, no one wants to take the responsibility or make the decision. So where does the 'buck stop'? It stops in the politician's or the bureaucrat's pocket.

America must elect its officials more and more on performance and less on promises. What we must see as a nation is that this corruption has seeped all the way down to the local level: school boards, town supervisors, our neighbors, us.

This condition of the breaking down of American society and culture is not just in Washington, D.C. It is on the increase in our schools, on our streets and in corporate life as well, but perhaps worst of all in family life, which I believe is the core of our current problems with crime and drugs. But at the heart of the problems in the family, in my opinion, is the loss or lack of a practicing Christian faith. The value system, or lack of it, originates in the home, and when that base is not secure and loving, society suffers. This is where we must get back to basics, stop the scramble for things and status. Stop this extreme self-seeking, where young people have to have romantic love maintained in the marriage or they break up, without appropriate owning up to the responsibility for the lives they have brought into the world. Next to divorce in destructiveness to the children is the lifestyle of a young couple who insist on having material things such as a modern house in the right neighborhood with new cars, etc., etc., to the extent that this require they both work in order to earn the income necessary to support this way of life. The kids come last, motherhood and keeping a home is looked down upon by today's feminists.

Children become latch-key kids, or are neglected or are 'bought-off' by parents too busy with business deals, golf, entertainment, cocktail parties, beer and sports – substituting money and things for love. These lifestyles won't work, as we are finding out. What's the answer? It is so simple and so easy and so rewarding, it makes one wonder if America is bewitched. The answer is love. BUT, even if we have the answer, does it do society any good? Some may be in a loving relationship with spouse, children and even parental families and siblings, and that's fine. It is not enough for America, because the love must spread to neighbors and even to people one does not like. This is impossible without a living God in our hearts, and if America is to be saved from going the way of Rome and Greece, she must once again enthrone the Christian God in its churches, its hearths and its hearts.

In the book, *Dead Right* by David Frum[4], the author puts it this way, "Are Americans drifting away from bourgeois individualism, with its emphasis on self-mastery, to expressive individualism and its cult of self-gratification? Do they insist too much upon their rights and heed too little their responsibilities? All of these faults can be laid at the door of religious America every bit as much as secular America." (p. 173) Many authors stress how much of the media have distorted our view of what is going on in America. Often the liberal left represents 'bleeding hearts' who want to give away other people's (the middle class) money for mismanaged welfare causes and other inappropriate and counter-productive dispensations. The conservative right, as well, often betray being puppets of the vested lobbyists of entrenched capitalistic interests (not the small or new entrepreneur, but rather the huge multi-national corporations).

It is also important to notice how the churches have, to a startling extent, abandoned their basic faith and principles. Take, for example, the televangelists who focus so much on money, caring little how they may be taking a 'widow's mite'. So many of the ministers are so impressed with worldly success of their wealthier members that few remember or care about Biblical admonitions to not be a respecter of persons, not to show favoritism to one that is finely dressed over another who can only afford the cheapest of suits or dresses. In other words, God is no respecter of persons and neither should we be, keeping in mind 'the last shall be first and the first last'. We have in large part become materialistic, name droppers, with a penchant not only for keeping up with the Joneses, but surpassing them. A very unchristian set of values; but then how many really believe in Jesus Christ as Savior and Redeemer and the only begotten Son of God? This may be a good clue to why so many feel there is no real purpose to mankind's existence.

Increasingly, the United States represents a nation by and large without the belief system of its founding fathers and a resignation from personal responsibility. This could very well be a result of a lack of vision or of a failure to make the effort to seek out God. More Americans need to take time out to dwell on ultimate meanings and to develop intimate meaningful relationships with their spouses. A fifty percent divorce rate sounds like a nation of juveniles who have to live in their own version of Hollywood 'bliss'; talk about VIRTUAL REALITY – this is the ultimate. From Olasky's well-researched book, *The Tragedy of American Compassion*[13], "The Mumbling Majority of the homeless, however, are men who are alone, who have been told that it is fine to be alone, and who have become used to receiving subsidy in their chosen lifestyle." (p. 212) "Many Americans have not attained this insight because they rely on the mediated compassion offered by journalists who are philosophically committed to Social Universalism and professionally involved with the production of sentimentality." (p. 213) Furthermore, he discovered the abiding necessity of a Christian-centered effort at those which were successful rehabilitation programs. We are at a critical juncture in our culture; it is time to hear the 'clarion call' and respond appropriately in our daily living and worship. *"And hath made of one blood all nations of men for to dwell on all the face of the earth, and hath determined the times before appointed, and the bounds of their habitation: That they should seek the Lord, if haply they might feel after Him, and find Him, though He be not far from every one of us: For in Him we live, and move, and have our being; as certain also of your own poets have said, For we are also His offspring."* (Acts 17:26-28)

Chapter 5
Those Who Don't Know That They Don't Know

The worst kind of ignorance is not to know that you are ignorant; in other words, to think you know all there is to know about a subject, or all that is worth knowing, when you don't. This is the case of so many humans who won't look beyond this life or think about the meaning and purpose of the human condition but focus all their efforts on pleasure and the acquisition of things – just living for the day or materialistic short term goals. *"I know thy works, that thou art neither cold nor hot: I would thou wert cold or hot. So then because thou art lukewarm, and neither cold nor hot, I will spue thee out of My mouth. Because thou sayest, I am rich, and increased with goods, and have need of nothing; and knowest not that thou art wretched, and miserable, and poor, and blind, and naked:"* (Revelation 3:15-17)

Perhaps more to be pitied are those of the 'elite' who are 'learned', but in reality, have minds and hearts closed by pride or ambition and who are really very prejudiced without knowing or accepting it. This type may be 'religious' – even ecclesiastics; pride and ambition are no respecters of person, class or calling. These are more to be pitied because as Christ said, *"But he that knew not, and did commit things worthy of stripes, shall be beaten with few stripes. For unto whomsoever much is given, of him shall be much required: and to whom men have committed much, of him they will ask the more."* (Luke 12:48)

Denying yourself and taking up your cross and following Christ can be done without being a fanatic or calling attention to yourself. Even yet today, a young father can still live in the world and provide for his children without inflicting unrealistic demands upon his children, so that they would be ostracized by their peers. This is because the Holy Spirit of God is still in the world keeping reasonable order, not allowing the full force of chaos and evil to take over. Even our 'carnal' society can only function as long as there are more people who are trustworthy and honest than those who are not. Civilization depends upon reasonable trust and honesty. A Christian must be scrupulously honest and trustworthy and obey the law and the authorities. How does that get him into trouble? He worships God in private and with other Christians. He is non-judgmental except, of course, when he must exercise judgment as to what is good or bad for his family and their health and welfare and their Christian faith; however, he is not judgmental in reference to the goodness or badness of someone else in terms of their salvation.

It is most necessary, however, to pray, read the Bible and to continually seek guidance from the Holy Spirit and our conscience. God works through human minds giving individuals inspiration in living and in careers. There is no reason we should not use what modern society has developed, such as medical treatments and educational institutions; however, it is important to keep in mind that all these things deal with the carnal and physical world in which we live and are not to supplant our dependence and guidance from God. Once again, two examples of carnal theories that may confuse more than help ascertain the 'truth' spiritually are evolution and psychology. To illustrate, concepts of psychology may seem to explain some actions such as irrational anger or a phobic response and thus, in turn, help the individual to bring certain behaviors or moods under control. Nevertheless, it is still an illusion and does not really explain psychopathology, nor does it provide relief, control and health in the final analysis – because it is carnal and not spiritual.

At some point, whether the person is a Christian or not, the 'defect' or 'disease' must be seen and understood as physical and carnal with the cure residing in the spiritual realm. Only in the spiritual does perfection and immortality reside. And some of these physical applications and treatments, whereas they may be helpful on the fleshly level and often help the Christian to function better in the world, are to be viewed for what they are, and what they are not. The same applies for medicine and drugs, often helpful on the physical plane but carrying the danger of confusing or misleading the Christian (or anyone) if over-generalization occurs. Psychologists know that often over-generalization can result in neurosis. We must be able to discern differences and to think and respond rather than to just react. The ultimate healer is God and the ultimate life is of God and from God and is God.

The question comes up, does God bless us carnally? This is incongruous. He may allow our lifestyle to be lavish, prosperous or powerful, but this may not be a spiritual blessing. It may be a spiritual testing; it certainly makes it harder for a person to keep his spiritual focus and perspective if he is surrounded with wealth, power, fame or talent. It may even be a seduction of the devil. We are here on earth in this fleshly, mortal and carnal existence to become spiritually minded through loving God and our fellow man and becoming self-less. The road upon which we are given to travel this journey may be with a broken or defective body, or with an impatient, ambitious nature or personality, we may be poor or rich, we may never succeed at anything in this world nor seem to make much of a difference in existing. BUT, the only real meaning to a human life is in becoming that perfect spiritual essence that God created from the beginning as Man and Woman – no matter how the world sees us, no matter how we are judged carnally, and perhaps most importantly, no matter how we judge who we are! We may feel that we are too worthless for God to care about us, which is not true. This perception either comes from the devil wanting to keep us defeated, or it ironically stems from self-preoccupation.

One of the things that psychology can offer us is a new way to view who we are and give us a psychological view of where our self-image comes from. Psychological explanation may be helpful even if it is not totally accurate, because it may help in overcoming the rejection of who we are. The next task, and even more important, is to distinguish our selves from our identity. We are each one of us a unique individual, but we must separate out self from our identity with God, Who is the only true Self.

Christ does want us to deny our carnal selves, but that is very different from rejecting or hating who we are. Satan uses self-doubt and self-hate as one more way to defeat and destroy humans, in addition to doing his best to make us doubt or reject God's existence or nature. During the weekly program 'Booknotes' on C-Span, (June 25,1995) Brian Lamb (the founder of C-Span) was interviewing Norman Mailer during which Mr. Mailer said, "Self-pity is the ultimate spiritual disease. Because that is anger against God. It shows lack of respect toward God." A very provocative statement, one worth some thought. Traditionally, pride is considered a deadly sin, because it is rebellion against God. Jesus leapfrogs the incompleteness and self-centeredness of psychology by asking us to deny ourselves and love others. This leads to real acceptance of who we are. Even though that sounds like a contradiction in terms, it is more like a paradox. Nevertheless, many psychological approaches can give us different viewpoints so that we can perhaps view who we are and, ultimately, God in a more positive way, and begin to grow spiritually. You may have to extricate yourself from the quicksand of self-loathing before you can walk on the plain of loving others. God is able to help us in many ways and to make use even of worldly things. *"And we know that all things work together for good to them that love God, to them who are the called according to His purpose."* (Romans 8:28)

There are many theories in psychology, and some of them often prove to be effective working hypotheses to the benefit of the client. As an example, the following is a quote from a provocative book by Lynch[11], ". . . Because of certain life experiences and an inability to live comfortably in one's own body, a person tends to believe that his or her adult world – that is, body – is not worth inviting others into. . . The greater the emotional pain, the more one becomes isolated from one's own body; and the more intense ones' sense of loneliness and disconnection, the more difficult it is to engage in real talk – that is, to be inviting. In an effort to protect themselves from this dilemma, these patients seal off their social membrane. Instead of being semi-permeable and shared, it becomes an impenetrable barrier, and their speech becomes an act of battering or hiding, rather than an invitation." (p. 243) With psychology, we may improve ourselves and our chances of relating to others and have a happier carnal life, but to strive after the real meaning of human life, that is, to become more like that perfect spiritual essence which God created can only be done through Jesus Christ and with the help of the Holy Spirit. Even so, we keep falling short and failing (at least this is my experience) and yet God keeps loving us. This impresses us, God's love and patience generates our love toward Him. *"We love Him, because He first loved us."* (1 John 4:19) God blesses us with love, joy, peace, longsuffering (patience), gentleness, goodness, faith, meekness (humility), and temperance (these are the real 'unalienable' spiritual human rights). What wonderful gifts. Few psychologists, psychiatrists or psychoanalysts can help very many of their patients secure even a few of these to any significant and abiding degree, through psychology alone.

However, the clergy should be a great help in this direction. And yet, despite a growing need, many of the clergy appear to have lost that living faith which can turn people toward God and spirituality (in the Christian sense). They often hand out pabulum, not because the congregation can't digest 'meat' but because these ministers do not have the strength of faith in what they are preaching and praying about to others. Thus, it often becomes a case of 'the blind leading the blind'.

Any person that seeks psychotherapy from a clinical psychologist can 'learn' in a carnal way where his problems come from and he can be told what to do to change for the better, but the change is entirely up to him. He is alone in his battle, unless he sees it from a spiritual point of view and seeks spiritual help from the Holy Spirit. However, he may not even get carnal insight from the psychologist, but the sessions may be mainly 'the purchase of friendship'. If he seeks help from a psychiatrist, he most likely will be given a drug that may alleviate the symptoms but still won't get at the real problem. Finally, if he seeks out a psychoanalyst then, depending upon his financial means, he may devote 50 minutes anywhere from once a week to 4 or 5 times a week at a cost of from $5,000 to $50,000 a year for years. What a loss if it is merely in order to narcissistically be the center of two people's attention (maybe only one, most of the time) for the better part of an hour. As a result, becoming more mired in carnality (self) than ever. Psychology is the interpretation of the conversion into personal meaning of the physical stimuli, through the senses, of experiences, and can be the carnal substitute or counterfeit of the spiritual, (e.g., by confusing or substituting personal will and personal self for God's).

Religion can be the 'wolf in sheep's clothing' of the spiritual. Science is fine to improve physical life in a carnal world when it remains science and is value-neutral; it becomes a snare and a delusion when it is worshipped or when it brings about the worship of a human or humans.

"Humble yourselves there-fore under the mighty hand of God, that He may exalt you in due time: Casting all your care upon Him; for He careth for you. Be sober, be vigilant; because your adversary the devil, as a roaring lion, walketh about, seeking whom he may devour: Whom resist stedfast in the faith, knowing that the same afflictions are accomplished in your brethren that are in the world. But the God of all grace, Who hath called us unto His eternal glory by Christ Jesus, after that ye have suffered a while, make you perfect, stablish, strengthen, settle you. To Him be glory and dominion for ever and ever. Amen." (1 Peter 5:6-11)

In order to love God with all our heart, mind and soul; and to love our neighbors instead of our selves while on this earth, and in this physical state of being, we must constantly keep trying, no matter how often we fail or fall back, to put our reliance on and our trust in Jesus Christ and the Holy Spirit (not in our self). It is impossible to please God without faith and a Christian believes that no man can come to God except through Jesus Christ. When we recognize and accept the gift of faith and begin perceiving the TRUTH, we realize that physical existence on this earth is temporal, the end of which is death and ultimate destruction of the earth.

"But the day of the Lord will come as a thief in the night; in

which the heavens shall pass away with a great noise, and the elements shall melt with fervent heat, the earth also and the works that are therein shall be burned up." (2 Peter 3:10) *"Nevertheless we, according to His promise, look for new heavens and a new earth, wherein dwelleth righteousness."* (2 Peter 3:13) *"To whom God would make known what is the riches of the glory of this mystery among the Gentiles; which is Christ in you, the hope of glory."* (Colossians 1:27)

The really difficult thing to grasp and to accept is that we cannot do this through our own efforts AND that God will really help us – this does take time to perceive because God's way is not often our way. We were, in the beginning, created after His image and therefore our essence, both as man and woman, were perfect and immortal. Something beyond our current grasp happened and mankind found himself on a physical earth with a mortal body and a sinful nature. Mankind, on earth, is not by nature good but rather is sinful. He must correct this, but can only do so through Jesus Christ and with the Holy Spirit. Mankind's existence as perfect and immortal must continuously reflect the essence of God, and if ever he assumes that the essence is his, and self is inserted between God and himself, he instantly loses the essence of God and becomes mortal, temporal and sinful. The only way to get back to God is through Jesus Christ, with constant struggle until he dies, in Christ, and is resurrected upon Christ's return to this earth. The struggle is tremendous and is literally a matter between mortal death on earth and immortal life with God. Perhaps the reason 'the way' on earth is so important and difficult, I believe, is that when we go to 'glory' there will never be another usurpation of God. We (those who put on the new man) will finally be dead to the self and alive in Christ (God's essence) forever.

Thinking of possible reasons behind the human dilemma and struggle, because the mind wants everything to be rational and orderly, can be a trap in itself. It is enough to accept the 'fact' that man is basically sinful and capable of incredible evil, just because God says so. However, also just look around you, look at history, look at the world today – **allow your eyes to be opened**. God has given us a chance of redemption, through Jesus Christ taking our sinful nature on Himself and dying for us. He defeated evil, death and Satan, and rose from the dead and has sent us the Holy Spirit to make it possible for us to also triumph over sin and death, through Him. *"But now ye also put off all these: anger, wrath, malice, blasphemy, filthy communication out of your mouth. Lie not one to another, seeing that ye have put off the old man with his deeds; And have put on the new man, which is renewed in knowledge after the image of Him that created him: Where there is neither Greek nor Jew, circumcision nor uncircumcision, Barbarian, Scythian, bond nor free: but Christ is all, and in all. Put on, therefore, as the elect of God, holy and beloved, bowels of mercies, kindness, humbleness of mind, meekness, longsuffering; Forbearing one another, and forgiving one another, if any man have a quarrel against any: even as Christ forgave you, so also do ye. And above all these things put on charity, which is the bond of perfectness. And let the peace of God rule in your hearts, to the which also ye are called in one body; and be ye thankful."* (Colossians 3:8-15) What strength and help we can derive from the Bible. *"Wait on the Lord; be of good courage and He shall strenthen thine heart: wait, I say, on the Lord."* (Psalms 27:14) *". . . Not by might nor by power, but by My Spirit saith the Lord of Hosts!"* (Zechariah 4:6) *"Be still, and know that I am God: I will be exalted among the heathen, I will be exalted in the earth."* (Psalms 46:10)

We must keep in mind that we are **receptors** (see Matthew 16:15-19 and Matthew 16:21-23) and must seek and remain open to God's will. If we don't, we then eventually are complying with the devil's will as we have no independent will of our own; we are only free to choose, otherwise we are in rebellion and pawns of the devil, and thus receptors of Satan. If we don't seem to know what is God's will then we do our best and we do it in faith, if we have strong doubts and feel uneasy about our choice, then we don't do it. Whatever we do, we either do it 'knowing' it is God's will or we do it in faith otherwise, as I read the Bible, it is sin. You may not appear to be much in the eyes of the world, you most likely will not be one of the major actors on the stage of the world – or even in your own home town! *"For ye see your calling, brethren, how that not many wise men after the flesh, not many mighty, not many noble, are called:"* (1 Corinthians 1:26) *"For ye are dead, and your life is hid with Christ in God."* (Colossians 3:3) Will you choose **ACTUAL REALITY** or not? There is no in-between. With faith you know that you don't know, but you believe and trust and allow others to do the same – without judging them.

Chapter 6
Actual Reality vs. Virtual Reality

Mankind has now developed what is called a 'virtual reality' whereby, through the use of computers, software and headsets, a 'player' is able to enter into scenes displayed on a monitor, controlling a representation of himself. He can actually manipulate scenes and actions as well as other 'actors' in the 'game', within limits devised by the programmers of the software. The 'player' can rescue and win the heart of a beautiful woman, he can explore space, discover lost cities and hidden treasures, become a 400 hitter in baseball, etc. But when the 'game' is over, he has to take off the headset, the computer shuts off and he leaves the arcade where he paid his $25.00 to play and, alas, step back into his own reality, which may be returning to a tenement in the slums, or to a lonely and isolated life in a big city highrise. A dictionary (I.B.M. Dictionary of Computing 1993) definition of Virtual Reality: "a computer generated simulation of reality with which user can interact using specialized peripherals such as data gloves and head-mounted computer graphic displays. Synonymous with artificial reality."[9]

Now, God has stepped into our VIRTUAL REALITY of human life, day to day living on the stage of earth, in the form of Jesus Christ. Because He is omnipresent, omniscient and omnipotent, He has not left His universe as He is present throughout it, continuously 'running' it, in His **ACTUAL REALITY** of the perfect and eternal Universe. Our human earthly life is temporary – time limited in which we can strut and deceive and 'control' others and steal and cheat and 'win' and in general, to varying degrees, engorge our egos. However, to live that way is more than a waste of time; it is fatal, mortal, and may lead to a dire reality, after the 'game' of life is over and, if you are not present with God after this life, if you do still exist, you may 'exist' with Satan in his 'hell'. But Jesus Christ has shown us what kind of a life to live and thoughts to think while we are in our VIRTUAL REALITY of earthly, physical existence. So that when this VIRTUAL REALITY is over, we pass over into immortality and the **ACTUAL REALITY** of God's presence, which transcends all the euphoria and ecstasy we could ever have experienced on earth – and it continues forever. In other words, earthly life is to heavenly life as VIRTUAL REALITY is to **ACTUAL REALITY**.

"For many are called, but few are chosen." (Matthew 22:14) *"What is man, that Thou art mindful of him? and the son of man, that Thou visitest him? For Thou hast made him a little lower than the angels, and hast crowned him with glory and honour."* (Psalm 8:4-5) It appears clear that there is a hierarchy in the spiritual realm, reinforced by Christ choosing twelve disciples (God chose twelve tribes in the Old Testament as He also chose leaders, prophets and kings throughout Biblical history). Furthermore, I surmise this to be reinforced by the report that Jesus had 'favorites' among His chosen apostles. *"And I say also unto thee, That thou art Peter, and upon this rock I will build My church; and the gates of hell shall not prevail against it."* (Matthew 16:18) *"And after six days Jesus taketh Peter, James, and John his brother, and bringeth them up into an high mountain apart,"* (Matthew 17:1) *"Now there was leaning on Jesus' bosom one of His disciples, whom Jesus loved."* (Matthew 13:23) And there are other instances throughout the Bible of this type of selection; for example, David would fall into a very select group as would Enoch, Abraham, Moses and Elijah to mention a few.

It is possible that when Jesus said as above, *"For many are called, but few are chosen"*, He was referring to being chosen as Spiritual leaders (saints) to some varying degrees, rather than to the salvation of believers. *"Unto the church of God which is at Corinth, to them that are sanctified in Christ Jesus, called to be saints, with all that in every place call upon the name of Jesus Christ our Lord, both theirs and ours:"* (1 Corinthians 1:2) If this vein of thought is followed, then one could view the Bible (especially the New Testament) as a manual for Spiritual leaders (saints) and not so used by the average believer. In fact, this may be one of the important distinguishing characteristics that divides people into the two groups, that of saints and of believers, and is voluntary in choice and is not necessarily (and perhaps even, not usually) formal in nature. This line of thinking comes about in the struggle to place the Bible in the scheme of things. For it is obvious, to me at least, that there are three choices in this matter. Either the Bible is: 1) literally, the Word of God and must be taken in its entirety at face value; or 2) containing the Word of God, which must be interpreted to each human individually by the Holy Spirit. The remaining choice is 3) to regard it as uninspired and simply containing the wisdom of many wise men over the ages.

My choice, finally, after 66 years of wrestling with this matter (since the age of 8) is the second view. *"Study to shew thyself approved unto God, a workman that needeth not to be ashamed, rightly dividing the word of truth."* (2 Timothy 2:15) *"But God hath revealed them unto us by His Spirit: for the Spirit searcheth all things, yea, the deep things of God."* (1 Corinthians 2:10) *"Forasmuch as ye are manifestly declared to be the epistle of Christ ministered by us, written not with ink, but with the Spirit of the living God; not in tables of stone, but in fleshy tables of the heart."* (2 Corinthians 3:3) Since the Bible was handed down at first by word of mouth from one generation to the next and later was written and passed on, there is the possibility of error in just the transmitting of the message. Add to this the fact that some parts got lost or partially damaged, and restoration had to be done at times, and finally, we have the difficulty of translating from one language to another. As if this wasn't enough, men may have had different interpretations of events and instructions so that there is the likelihood of error creeping in without imputing deceit or manipulation. However, it could be very well that the first view is the 'correct' one and that certainly God would be able to maintain His Bible intact and accurate if He chose and perhaps He so chose; it would still require guidance from the Holy Spirit and only those whom He chose to receive His truth would be able to see or hear it.

I believe God wants us and, in fact, makes it necessary for us, to use our wonderful brain and free choice to not only revere and study the Bible, but also to seek His present guidance through the Holy Spirit to accommodate to seeming contradictions within the Bible itself and to help clarify obtuse and difficult passages. We should understand that we must respect other's understanding of Biblical passages that differ from our own interpretation. There is no justification for a Christian to impose his belief verbatim on another. There is always room for growing and learning, and when the effort is sincere and tempered by experience and wisdom, we should not arrive at radically different interpretations, certainly never to the degree of killing one another over fine-tuning in our interpretations. In fact, St.Paul instructs us, *"Let nothing be done through strife or vainglory; but in lowliness of mind let each esteem other better than themselves."* (Philippians 2:3) *"Do all things without murmurings and disputings: That ye may be blameless and harmless, the sons of God, without rebuke, in the midst of a crooked and perverse nation, among whom ye shine as lights in the world; Holding forth the word of life; that I may rejoice in the day of Christ, that I have not run in vain, neither laboured in vain."* (Philippians 2:14-16) *"But avoid foolish questions, and genealogies, and contentions, and strivings about the law; for they are unprofitable and vain."* (Titus 3:9)

Human beings have a God that entered into His own creation, became one of us and dwelt among us. He walked upon the earth within a sequence of time! He showed us the way He wanted us to live and He fought and defeated Satan in Satan's realm – this world of non-faith, disobedience and carnality. He overcame Satan's 'creation': sin, time, evil, suffering and death. All this in the form of Jesus Christ. In other words, He showed us the **ACTUAL REALITY** of spiritual life as contrasted with our VIRTUAL REALITY of physical living. Since Jesus was resurrected, God has been with those whom He chooses in the form of the Holy Ghost (His Holy Spirit).

I believe it would then be those 'Spiritual leaders' (saints) who are still alive and are transformed at Christ's return, as well as those saints who were already dead by the time of His return, but would also be the one's that participate in the first resurrection. All the rest of the 'believers' would, thereafter, be judged, and if their names were in the Book of Life, would also achieve immortality. None of the aforementioned would suffer the second death and be cast into the fires of Hell. *"Blessed and holy is he that hath part in the first resurrection: on such the second death hath no power, but they shall be priests of God and of Christ, and shall reign with Him a thousand years."* (Revelation 20:6) *"And I saw the dead, small and great, stand before God; and the books were opened: and another book was opened, which is the book of life: and the dead were judged out of those things which were written in the books, according to their works. And the sea gave up the dead which were in it; and death and hell delivered up the dead which were in them: and they were judged every man according to their works. And death and hell were cast into the lake of fire, This is the second death. And whosoever was not found written in the book of life was cast into the lake of fire."* (Revelation 20:12-15)

There are many bad people in the world as well as evil ones. I suspect the evil ones do not change and that there are many who were bad at times in their lives, but became 'good' before they died. Those who had been 'good' during their lives, but ended up being bad, may yet avoid the second death when they are judged by God, perhaps, if the good outweighs the bad – only God can and will be the judge of that. Only the chosen spiritual leaders or saints would be those, I presume, who partake in the transformation or first resurrection and have no fear of the second death. The believers would also be spared from the second death whose names were found in the 'book of life'.

Heaven is not a city paved with gold; the glory of life (immortal) with God is unimaginable but we can very well appreciate, in part, how wonderful it will be in contrast to our present lives. *"And I saw a new heaven and a new earth: for the first heaven and the first earth were passed away; and there was no more sea."* (Revelation 21:1) *"And God shall wipe away all tears from their eyes; and there shall be no more death, neither sorrow, nor crying, neither shall there be any more pain: for the former things are passed away."* (Revelation 21:4) *"But the fearful, and unbelieving, and the abominable, and murderers, and whoremongers, and sorcerers, and idolaters, and all liars, shall have their part in the lake which burneth with fire and brimstone: which is the second death."* (Revelation 21:8)

Hereafter, I shall use the terms saints and believers in the sense that the former (saints) study the bible and progressively seek to be obedient to the Holy Spirit as the driving motivation of their lives and, further, that there is confirmation in their lives by the manifestation of 'the fruits of the spirit'. *"But the fruit of the Spirit is love, joy, peace, longsuffering, gentleness, goodness, faith, Meekness, temperance: against such there is no law."* (Galatians 5:22-23) I shall further assume that the latter (believers) acknowledge Jesus Christ as the Son of God and believe in Him as their Saviour, but are more consumed with daily living and trying to be a 'good' person than in being in tune with the Holy Spirit and studying to make themselves 'workmen' unto God. *"Study to shew thyself approved unto God, a workman that needeth not to be ashamed, rightly dividing the word of truth."* (2 Timothy 2:15) The foregoing represents my belief at this stage of my spiritual development. It would be a mistake, however, to think that one can substitute studying the Bible and praying, for living one's faith. *"Even so faith, if it hath not works, is dead, being alone."* (James 2:17)

The above division into saints and believers does not necessarily follow along the lines of the clergy versus laymen. Remember Christ's words, *"But many that are first shall be last; and the last shall be first."* (Matthew 19:30) My use of saints does not refer to one canonized by the Catholic Church. It is most important that believers strive to become saints. *"Now therefore ye are no more strangers and foreigners, but fellowcitizens with the saints, and of the household of God; And are built upon the foundation of the apostles and prophets, Jesus Christ Himself being the chief corner stone; In Whom all the building fitly framed together groweth unto an holy temple in the Lord: In Whom ye also are builded together for an habitation of God through the Spirit."* (Ephesians 2:19-22) *"That Christ may dwell in your hearts by faith; that ye, being rooted and grounded in love, May be able to comprehend with all saints what is the breadth, and length, and depth, and height; And to know the love of Christ, which passeth knowledge, that ye might be filled with all the fulness of God."* (Ephesians 3:17-19) *"And He gave some, apostles; and some, prophets; and some, evangelists; and some, pastors and teachers; For the perfecting of the saints, for the work of the ministry, for the edifying of the body of Christ: Till we all come in the unity of the faith, and of the knowledge of the Son of God, unto a perfect man, unto the measure of the stature of the fulness of Christ:"* (Ephesians 4:11-13)

God obviously created us with, not only free choice, but an astounding brain capable of intricate reasoning, logic, experimentation, inspiration, discovery and also of free independent thinking. This being the case, it would hardly seem that believers could not distinguish between common sense and blind obedience to evil, or between faith and fanaticism, nor further between good and evil, between ego or pride and selfless love. Thus, it is not necessary and probably not the Catholic Church's intention for believers to give God's place over to the Pope (God's Holy Spirit can communicate to us without the necessity of an intercessor).

It offends the God-given right of free choice to support a dictator or to use denial and ulterior motives in interpreting the Bible to fit a fanatic's objectives. Belonging in this category are those who use the ends to justify the means, those who would deny our freedom because they want to control us for their own purposes. Man is not inherently good (contrary to many liberal's belief) and contrary to many conservatives belief, success and profit are not sufficient 'ends' to justify questionable or destructive 'means'. It is only the presence of the Holy Spirit yet in this world that keeps the evil at bay. The saints and the believers are far out-numbered. Even so, God will be glorified and His will *will* be done and the good *will* be victorious. It is so blind if one has his or her focus on the here and now, on the material things that will perish with the physical body, when one could become spiritually minded and achieve immortality and eternal love, joy and peace. That is the difference between VIRTUAL REALITY and **ACTUAL REALITY**. *"These things I have spoken unto you, that in Me ye might have peace. In the world ye shall have tribulation: but be of good cheer; I have overcome the world."* (1 John 5:4)

Chapter 7
Cosmic Struggle Whose Reach Exceeds Our Grasp

For the sake of discussion, I will assume the following three basic statements to be true:

1) God exists, is good, loving and interested in each human being personally, He is eternal and will eventually be all and in all;
2) Satan exists, is evil, wants to destroy human beings, is time-bound and will eventually perish and disappear;
3) Man has free choice and is basically neutral but with an evil propensity for self-seeking and/or self-aggrandizement.

In the light of the preceding, I will 'logically' assume that there is a cosmic struggle between good and evil over man. That God will always be available to man to help him, forgive him, love him and win him over from Satan and evil. That God is spiritual and eternal, whereas Satan is mortal and carnal. Furthermore, man will tend to some degree to be one or a combination of the following:

A) self-centered and narcissistic;
B) selfish and grasping for land, money and 'things';
C) power-seeking and attempting to control others by any means;
D) lustful and consumed with sexual or perverse thoughts and actions;
E) lazy or gluttonous and non-productive;
F) hedonistic, sensual, pleasure-seeking.

The above seems to set the world stage pretty much the way it has been since recorded history. If I were to imagine myself, without Christ, in various types of surroundings and having great success, I suppose that I would not only be capable of falling deeply into one or more of the above categories, but actually be strongly attracted to that lifestyle. The Bible states that mainly the 'failures', the poor, the sickly, the lonely and the 'defective' would be those that mostly chose to seek out God – if any did, because the world is so alluring and man so self-centered and has great, great difficulty seeing beyond the here and now. Delay of gratification and intolerance of ambiguity are among the main culprits.

In the end, because free choice exists, man chooses his own destiny and ultimate condition. In a certain sense, however, we are 'elected' or 'predestinated' or 'chosen' because God is by definition all knowing; He will know from the time of each of our beginnings, which end each of us will ultimately choose. Thus even though we have freedom to choose, God with His foreknowledge of how each of us will ultimately decide our own destiny (spirituality and immortality or carnality and death), has already 'chosen' us. Thus election, pre-destination and being chosen is not something that we need to get 'hung-up' on or be overly concerned about. Like Nike says, 'Just do it!' Because man is a creation of God and in His image, albeit corrupted, he is able to invent, innovate and create things in the carnal world that increasingly simulate the spiritual order. As an example, now through telecommunications, he has been able to surmount distances and time to a great degree. Nevertheless, the real trademarks of spirituality, in aggregate, have not been significantly duplicated carnally, nor will they ever be. I am speaking of love, joy, peace, patience, gentleness, goodness, faith, humility and temperance; without these what good are all the modern scientific achievements or the pursuits of momentary gratifications?

There are persuasive misconceptions, but not of a substantive nature, for a lack of commitment to the spiritual: we cannot conceive of God, cannot grasp His essence; we are afraid that in giving up our 'self' we give up everything. If you stop and think about immortality for yourself, you may doubt whether you want to live forever (especially as you grow older or have serious health or personal problems). But if you accept Christ's salvation, you will have a new and perfect spiritual body for eternity. *"And God shall wipe away all tears from their eyes; and there shall be no more death, neither sorrow, nor crying, neither shall there be any more pain: for the former things are passed away. And He that sat upon the throne said, Behold, I make all things new. And He said unto me, Write: for these words are true and faithful. And He said unto me, It is done. I am Alpha and Omega, the beginning and the end. I will give unto him that is athirst of the fountain of the water of life freely. He that overcometh shall inherit all things; and I will be his God, and he shall be My son."* (Revelation 21:4-7) *"Nevertheless we, according to His promise, look for new heavens and a new earth, wherein dwelleth righteousness."* (2 Peter 3:13)

In fact, few people really think about or dwell upon concepts such as infinity, finiteness, nothing, eternity, the beginning before there was anything, the end after which there is nothing. Since we really cannot 'know' these things in the sense of knowing worldly things, all that most of us do is to name these concepts, and then the thought shuts down because these things are beyond our logic and physical experience. Truly, we may 'reach' for the comprehension of some things, whose experience is not only beyond our 'grasp' but even the understanding of them exceeds our ability to know. There are questions with answers and there are questions without answers, but the most important questions are the ones without answers but which have meaning. *"For we know in part, and we prophesy in part. But when that which is perfect is come, then that which is in part shall be done away. When I was a child, I spake as a child, I understood as a child, I thought as a child: but when I became a man, I put away childish things. For now we see through a glass, darkly; but then shall I know even as also I am known. And now abideth faith, hope, charity, these three; but the greatest of these is charity."* (1 Corinthians 13:9-13)

Christianity is elegant in its simplicity and reality orientation. No other philosophy or religion approaches its applicability to the solution of the human situation. But only one person has ever really lived in perfect compliance with its commandments. This, I feel, indicates that we humans are at the center of a titanic struggle between good and evil. We are so lacking in faith and unwilling to deny our 'right to ourselves' as Oswald Chambers[1] so often said, that we keep falling too short to provide any real convincing evidence of the power of faith and self-sacrifice. *"Jesus saith unto him, I am the way, the truth, and the life: no man cometh unto the Father, but by Me."* (John 14:6) *"And He said to them all, If any man will come after Me, let him deny himself, and take up his cross daily, and follow Me."* (Luke 9:23)

Satan especially targets those who are most earnestly trying to follow Christ. Despite this, many do live Christian lives, but not many others wish to follow after them because of their own preconceived notions. Others start out, but are defeated on the way. It seems that more and more, most never make any serious attempt to give anything but lip service. Increasingly, there are too many pleasant distractions or more immediately gratifying undertakings. So the bulk of people do not struggle with why we humans exist and whether there is any real purpose to life. It is easier just to think of being here in this world and to live strictly in the here and now, for the here and now. Psychology is often referred to as the new religion and psychologists as the new priests. Unfortunately, some Christian churches have, to varying degrees, become pseudo-psychological clinics where a 'feel good about yourself' atmosphere prevails. In some of the more fervent churches, there can be a very unchristian judgementalness toward 'outsiders'. However much this discourages others from looking more deeply into Christianity, it is not a legitimate excuse for any human being to neglect divining his true nature and purpose.

Actually, the existence of 'good' in this world is like a flower trying to survive in an untended garden. There are many bad people and some good people, but the majority are neither good nor bad, just uncommitted. Yet good doesn't die out; but in the end, God will have to intervene on behalf of the good and the termination of the evil. Still, does He hold off because there are people turning to good from bad and even some 'lukewarmers' becoming committed? No matter how few make this transformation through the Holy Spirit and Jesus Christ, will God wait and hold off, just as He held off with Sodom and Gomorrah? Adam failed in the very beginning of our race of humans and of the first two who were conventionally born, one (Cain) was bad, who murdered his brother, Abel.

God sent a series of great men, prophets and kings; and of all the nations, there was only one (Israel) and eventually of that, only one tribe that was good (Judah) and even in that tribe the tendency was always to turn toward evil. Finally, God Himself came down in human form (as Jesus Christ) and walked on this earth to show us how He wanted us to be and also to show us how much He loved us and how loving He was.

We are not to judge who is good or evil, nor are we to say any are beyond hope, no matter where in the world they exist, or in what culture they live. We are to discern between good and evil ways as far as our own thoughts, intentions or acts are concerned. The psychologist who says it doesn't matter what you think as long as you don't act on it – is WRONG. Because what we think about and dwell upon, we grow to lust after, and eventually it shapes what we do or become. *"Let no man say when he is tempted, I am tempted of God: for God cannot be tempted with evil, neither tempteth He any man: But every man is tempted, when he is drawn away of his own lust, and enticed. Then when lust hath conceived, it bringeth forth sin: and sin, when it is finished, bringeth forth death."* (James 1:13-15) Every man is tempted by his own lust, that means all of us, but we are to take heart and fight the good fight. *"Wherefore let him that thinketh he standeth take heed lest he fall. There hath no temptation taken you but such as is common to man: but God is faithful, Who will not suffer you to be tempted above that ye are able; but will with the temptation also make a way to escape, that ye may be able to bear it."* (1 Corinthians 10:12-13)

All of the helpful inventions, scientific and medical advances come from Divine inspiration. To think that these discoveries are spontaneously generated in the human mind is more ludicrous than the medieval belief (before Louis Pasteur) that germs spontaneously developed from nothing! God challenges us to prove our faith; we are our own 'laboratories'. Each person only knows himself and only partially at that!

We need to keep working at deepening our faith and manifesting it in our lives daily. *"And be not conformed to this world: but be ye transformed by the renewing of your mind that ye may prove what is that good, and acceptable, and perfect, will of God."* (Romans 12:2) Further, St. Paul tells the Corinthians, *"Examine yourselves, whether ye be in the faith; prove your own selves, how that Jesus Christ is in you, except ye be reprobates."* (2 Corinthians 13:5) And to the Galatians he wrote, *"For if a man think himself to be something, when he is nothing, he deceiveth himself. But let every man prove his own work, and then shall he have rejoicing in himself alone, and not in another. For every man shall bear his own burden."* (Galatians 6:3-5) Over and over again, St. Paul stresses that it is an on-going battle and that it is personal. *"Prove all things: hold fast that which is good."* (1 Thessalonians 5:21) *"And have put on the new man, which is renewed in knowledge after the image of Him that created him."* (Colossians 3:10)

It is so important to study the New Testament and to study it in deference to television, stereo, etc. This does not mean you can't have a normal life, but use diversions and distractions to moderation and be aware of how much time they take and how much more productive and fruitful your life could be with less entertainment. You could begin to experience abiding joy and an inner sense of peace and security instead of momentary 'pleasures' and a growing restlessness. One of the areas of most growth is in the area of security and inner peace. *"But we had the sentence of death in ourselves, that we should not trust in ourselves, but in God which raiseth the dead:"* (2 Corinthians 1:9) *"For our rejoicing is this, the testimony of our conscience, that in simplicity and godly sincerity, not with fleshly wisdom, but by the grace of God, we have had our conversation in the world, and more abundantly to You-ward."* (2 Corinthians 1:12)

Each of us has our separate journey, not necessarily or even usually alone. Nevertheless, in the final analysis, each of our outcomes is up to the individual. No one can save you except Jesus Christ and then only if you choose Him over yourself. That is where the battle is, with the self. It has been thus since Adam when he insisted on catering to his 'deluded want' rather than obeying God. Perhaps obedience training is a central part of becoming spiritual beings, but it is submission willingly and joyfully. The love that binds a good marriage is based on trust and respect and that is a good starting place as you read the Bible, i.e. read with an open mind being receptive and not stumbling over things you don't understand or disagree with at first. Because the nature of things are on a cosmic basis and there is a titanic struggle going on that we can't 'grasp' intellectually and we cannot 'reach' experientially. I quote from *The Magic Mirror of M. C. Escher*[2], "We find it impossible to imagine that somewhere beyond the furthest stars of the night sky there should come an end to space, a frontier beyond which there is nothing more. The notion of 'emptiness' does, of course, have some meaning for us, because a space can be empty, at all events conceptually, but our powers of imagination are incapable of encompassing the notion of 'nothing' in the sense of 'spacelessness'." (page 102)

We chose to eat of the fruit of the tree of the knowledge of good and evil in accordance to the 'will' of Satan and against the will of God. This is true because we (humans) are only **receptors**; we have no legitimate 'will' of our own. In fact, there is only one will in all of creation and that is the Will of God; the devil's 'will' is a counterfeit and the basis of our earthly VIRTUAL REALITY. But since Adam and Eve made that horribly rebellious choice, to disobey God and assume that they had a will of their own, they decided for all humans (except for those individuals with whom God interceded) until Jesus Christ freed us through His atonement and now we have freedom again to choose **GOD'S ACTUAL**

REALITY, which in fact, is the only reality. Thus, we do know the difference between good and evil and furthermore, we continue to know that difference – from birth – unless we blind ourselves and continue to deliberately sin until we become self-deceived. Therefore, until and unless that happens, we 'know' if and when we are choosing good or evil, in our thinking, talking and behaving, and we can, therefore, choose the good that is the will of God.

There is an exception, in my opinion, and that is a child that has been brought up by parents, warped in their own thinking, who have indoctrinated their child to believe in false tenets. In addition, young children who have been taught perverse sexual practices and/or violent lifestyles deliberately, or ones who have been malignantly abused or rejected, may be unable to know what is right or wrong – morally or spiritually. God can, however, open up that mind and conscience later.

Chapter 8
Wonderful Weakness

It is amazing the degree to which the New Testament promotes pacifism, acquiescence, compliance and unassertiveness. Read through the Gospels, Paul's Epistles and the writings of St. John. The Lord promotes turning the other cheek, going the second mile and loving your enemies – as a starter. St. Paul lists the fruits of the Spirit in terms of love, joy, peace, longsuffering, gentleness, goodness, faith, temperance and meekness. St. John extols purity, righteousness, truth and above all love, love, love. Where are courage, strength and resistance mentioned? Strength is used basically in the following sense, *"And He answering, said, Thou shalt love the Lord thy God with all thy heart, and with all thy soul, and with all thy strength, and with all thy mind; and thy neighbour as thyself."* (Luke 10:27) So there is no touting of machismo, the macho-man with biceps and brute strength or force. In Acts, St. Luke relates that St. Paul *". . . thanked God, and took courage."* (Acts 28:15) This is a different kind of courage than that of a soldier in battle or a football player. To resist is mentioned by St. James and others, who use it in basically the same context, *"Submit yourselves therefore to God. Resist the devil, and he will flee from you."* (James 4:7) This is no call to arms to fight other people or to be confrontational.

What then about the manly virtues of power and strength? I refer you to the following as illustrative of the theme running through the New Testament. *". . . My grace is sufficient for thee; for My strength is made perfect in weakness. . ."* (2 Corinthians 12:9) *"I can do all things through Christ which strengtheneth me."* (Philippians 4:13)

Power is used in another sense that is illuminating, *"Let every soul be subject unto the higher powers. For there is no power but of God: the powers that be are ordained of God. Whosoever therefore resisteth the power, resisteth the ordinance of God: and they that resist shall receive to themselves damnation."* (Romans

13:1-2) So, we are to be obedient to our rulers, but it is equally important to keep the proper New Testament perspective in mind. *"And Jesus answering said unto them, Render unto Caesar the things that are Caesar's, and to God the things that are God's. And they marvelled at Him."* (Mark 12:17)

One might pose the question, what if the ruler is evil (a Hitler, for example) and gives you an order such as turning over Jews to the authorities; or if you are a Jew, to submit being sent with your family to a concentration camp or a gas chamber? There can be all kinds of interpretations of this passage (Romans 13:1-2) or different translations of the original words that could indicate various degrees of application or alternate meanings. For example, one could say this is just referring to church leadership or authority that you must obey; or it could mean that you would suffer the wrath of the civil authorities and not of damnation. But let us assume the words and this translation at face value. We would, of course, not comply with an evil order or be the instruments of terror in the hands of an evil ruler and we would certainly try to escape persecution and injustice being imposed upon our family or ourselves. Our means, however, would be non-violent and passive resistance if at all possible. If, because of our lack of faith, we had to resort to physical violence in defense of ourselves or our family, we would. And, I believe that God would forgive a man if he killed another man who was trying to rape his wife. After all, He 'put away' David's heinous crime involving the killing of Bathsheba's husband, Uriah. Nevertheless, I do believe that if one has enough faith, God may deliver one's loved ones out of danger just as He delivered Abraham's nephew, Lot, and his family out of the destruction of Sodom. (God may not, depending on His plans, which at times are incomprehensible to the human – but rest assured ultimate good is being accomplished.) Still, our mind set should be, according to St. Paul, as follows, *"Be not overcome of evil, but overcome evil with good."* (Romans 12:21)

This element of Christianity must be more fully explored. The New Testament position on this is very emphatic and unequivocal as is evident in the following, *"Ye have heard that it hath been said, An eye for an eye, and a tooth for a tooth: But I say unto you, That ye resist not evil: but whosoever shall smite thee on thy right cheek, turn to him the other also. And if any man will sue thee at the law, and take away thy coat, let him have thy cloak also. And whosoever shall compel thee to go a mile, go with him twain."* (Matthew 5:38-41) *"But I say unto you, Love your enemies, bless them that curse you, do good to them that hate you, and pray for them which despitefully use you, and persecute you; That ye may be the children of your Father which is in heaven: for He maketh His sun to rise on the evil and on the good, and sendeth rain on the just and on the unjust. For if ye love them which love you, what reward have ye? do not even the publicans the same? And if ye salute your brethren only, what do ye more than others? do not even the publicans so? Be ye therefore perfect, even as your Father which is in heaven is perfect."* (Matthew 5:44-48)

When they came to arrest Jesus, one of his disciples drew his sword to defend Jesus, *"Then Jesus said unto him, Put up again thy sword into its place: for all they that take the sword shall perish with the sword. Thinkest thou that I cannot now pray to My Father, and He shall presently give Me more than twelve legions of angels?"* (Matthew 26:52-53) Near the end of His earthly, physical life when Pilate was judging Him, *"Jesus answered, My kingdom is not of this world: if my kingdom were of this world, then would My servants fight, that I should not be delivered to the Jews: but now is My kingdom not from hence."* (John 18:36) He also says; blessed are the meek, the merciful, and the peacemakers. It is summed up, *"Therefore, all things whatsoever ye would that men should do to you do ye even so to them: for this is the law and the prophets."* (Matthew 7:12) To reinforce this non-aggressiveness further, *"Behold, I send you forth as sheep in the midst of wolves: be ye therefore wise as serpents, and harmless as doves."* (Matthew 10:16) *"And fear not them which kill the body, but are not able to kill the soul: but rather fear Him which is able to destroy both soul and body in hell."* (Matthew 10:28) *"He that findeth his life shall lose it: and he that loseth his life for My sake shall find it."* (Matthew 10:39)

True Christianity is not a 'zero-sum game' (a game in which the cumulative winnings equal the cumulative losses); it is an all or nothing matter. *"For to me to live is Christ, and to die is gain."* (Philippians 1:21) *"For none of us liveth to himself, and no man dieth to himself. For whether we live, we live unto the Lord; and whether we die, we die unto the Lord: whether we live therefore, or die, we are the Lord's. For to this end Christ both died, and rose, and revived, that He might be Lord both of the dead and living."* (Romans 14:7-9) We are to stake our very lives upon our faith, and our faith cannot be proven or it is no longer faith – by definition. As stated previously, to 'prove' faith is an oxymoron.

The above is further evidence of how central a part faith plays in our lives and why it is so difficult to live Christian faith. But then why not? It is what this life is all about – receiving and demonstrating faith – without which we cannot please God. And since this is one of the foundations of achieving immortal life with Christ, why wouldn't it be so demanding? Look at the reward! That sounds as if we are to earn our salvation, but no, it is a gift from God – but a gift we either choose to accept and manifest or we deny and reject. As St. Paul states, *"I can do all things through Christ which strengtheneth me."* (Philippians 4:13)

I think that being 'born again' is a birth and then a growth process which, for most of us, takes whatever lifetime is allotted to each of us, and that even then we are not perfect because we do not have perfect faith. We do not live enough in the Holy Spirit, even though we accept Christ and know that of ourselves we can do nothing. We do not call upon Him enough. Thus, in the end, we can only live in hope that through God's mercy, love and grace we will receive salvation and immortality through Jesus Christ. We are an accomplished work already in Christ. (See Romans 7:14-25) So life has meaning and there is purpose to our lives. God's Holy Spirit is with us to the degree that it is important to us to be Christians without a vested interest. That is, Christians, because it is the life of Christ that we want to emulate, since His Spirit has opened our eyes, minds, hearts and souls (and not because it gives us power, stature or a livelihood). We see how empty a natural life lived only for the here and now really is, not only for us but for our children and loved ones. This motivation is a gift from God, unearned and unwarranted by any of us.

Turning to the Old Testament, we read, "*. . . Not by might, nor by power, but by My Spirit, saith the Lord of Hosts.*" (Zechariah 4:6) Further, "*Be still and know that I am God: I will be exalted among the heathen, I will be exalted in the earth.*" (Psalm 46:10) "*Wait on the Lord: be of good courage, and He shall strengthen thine heart: wait, I say, on the Lord.*" (Psalm 27:14) And finally, "*Truly my soul waiteth upon God: from Him cometh my salvation. He only is my rock and my salvation; He is my defence; I shall not be greatly moved.*" (Psalm 62:1-2) Back to the New Testament, "*For in Him we live, and move, and have our being; as certain also of your own poets have said, For we are also His offspring.*" (Acts 17:28) This quotation is taken from a very illuminating context where St. Paul was preaching to Greeks in Athens. It is plain that all men everywhere have been called in all the world; see especially Acts chapter 17, verses 18 through 32. The vital thing is to have faith and to live in it, not to merely pay lip service and go through the motions of being 'religious'. "*Having a form of godliness, but denying the power thereof: from such turn away. For of this sort are they which creep into houses, and lead captive silly women laden with sins, led away with divers lusts. Ever learning, and never able to come to the knowledge of the truth.*" (2 Timothy 3:5-7)

Striving to make your faith real is worthy of a lifetime's effort of whatever length the Lord assigns to you. **This being the case, Satan's biggest arena of battle over your soul is to make you doubt.** Doubt God's existence and love, doubt that you are called, doubt that you have faith. After all, that was the avenue Satan used with Eve in the Garden of Eden and he has been using it ever since. It probably would not be far off the mark to say that the bigger battles you have with doubt, the more vital is your faith. Do not let doubt discourage you, but rather seek God more, in prayer, in reading the Bible and in living your faith. *"For by grace are ye saved through faith; and that not of yourselves: it is the gift of God."* (Ephesians 2:8)

Logic and rationality derive from facts, observations and experience, from which premises are based that form the foundations of different logical systems. Then, they must be 'tested' to see if they 'work' in the 'real' world. For example, in science, sending a man to the moon successfully confirmed many theories of mathematics and physics. In addition, the logical process may serve some useful psychological purpose, such as quelling a panic stemming from chaotic conditions – even though the thought process may not represent reality and may be based on a false premise. For example, the child of neglectful or abusive parents may very well be in a state of panic over the possibility of a capricious parent abandoning him (to starve to death) or killing him in a fit of rage. The child cannot cope with anything else (such as school, athletics, socializing) as long as his brain is taken up with this terror. So, at some level in his brain, the 'brilliant' premise (false though it is) is made to the effect that daddy is not bad, I am; so if I am good, he will be good. Even if the child is good and the father still treats him the same, the panic is quelled – because the child now has 'control' (that is, if he is good, he won't be neglected or beaten) even though this is not true. (He may have rationalized, 'I am not good enough' or he may stop short of 'being good', that is, not really test his belief.) He can now deny the reality because it 'makes sense'. Unfortunately, when he grows up, he becomes an adult that cannot commit to close relationships because down deep is the belief that he is bad or unlovable.

Since often, we do not have all the facts or accurate observations, our premises and consequent reasoning are limited, but they can be subject to change when more data or different data are introduced, if we are still receptive and open-minded instead of having closed our mind and denying any 'new' reality or information.

For example, compare Galileon or Euclidian physics and/or mathematics with those of Einstein. In the example of the little boy cited above, new data (e.g. a woman that loves him and is kind to him) often does not change the underlying fear or negative self-image because it has become a conditioned response by now, and has been repressed because the 'truth' is so unbearable. The tragedy is that the 'truth' was a lie and the reality is that he is lovable and 'good'.

Accordingly, our limited types of thought and observational processes are not in a position to disprove God's existence or establish His nature, nor are we in a position to know His plans or purpose for mankind. This makes it more comprehensible why it is that faith is such a basic tenet in pleasing God. It does also make us acknowledge our limitations and hopefully humble us somewhat.

God gave us free choice, that is, the ability to disobey, when He told us not to eat of the fruit of the tree of the knowledge of good and evil. But we disobeyed (sinned) and ate; many consequences of an adverse nature followed that act. From then on, we also had to develop judgment to discriminate between good and evil. Out of the crucible of free choice, faith can be accepted and grow. In the process, judgment is acquired between good and evil – not judgmentalness as to the worthiness of another person in God's order of things. Finally, God's love flows in and results in true rebirth, all of this done only in the presence of hope. But what hope? Our hope is for a new life, for a new world and for a new human nature. And what is the basis for our hope? Jesus Christ.

And therein lies our victory, as St. Paul writes, *"And He said unto me, My grace is sufficient for thee: for My strength is made perfect in weakness. Most gladly therefore will I rather glory in my infirmities, that the power of Christ may rest upon me. Therefore I take pleasure in infirmities, in reproaches, in necessities, in persecutions, in distresses for Christ's sake: for when I am weak, then am I strong."* (2 Corinthians 12:9-10) What a wonderful weakness! *"Since ye seek a proof of Christ speaking in me, which to you-ward is not weak, but is mighty in you. For though He was crucified through weakness, yet He liveth by the power of God. For we also are weak in Him, but we shall live with Him by the power of God toward you."* (2 Corinthians 13:3-4)

"And He said, Go Forth, and stand upon the mount before the Lord, And behold, the Lord passed by, and a great and strong wind rent the mountains and brake in pieces the rocks before the Lord; but the Lord was not in the earthquake; And after the earthquake a fire; but the Lord was not in the fire: and after the fire a still small voice; And it was so, when Elijah heard it, that he wrapped his face in his mantle, and went out, and stood in the entering in of the cave. And, behold, there came a voice unto him, and said, What doest thou here, Elijah?" (1 Kings 19:11-13)

Chapter 9
From Essence to Existence to Perfection

The matter of good and evil in the world, the extent of it and the seeming unresponsiveness, at times, on the part of God, leads me to speculate about the order of things. So what follows is a scenario that might make sense, but be untrue and fall far wide of the mark. We are not capable of understanding or encompassing God's plan, and so the bottom line is always that God is goodness, is righteousness, is justice, is love and was embodied on our earthly plane in the form of Jesus Christ, and is always present with all who worship Him – in the form of the Holy Spirit. God made us, man and woman, at the same time and we were made in His likeness, and He declared us good like the rest of His creation.

"And God said, Let Us make man in Our image, after Our likeness: and let them have dominion over the fish of the sea, and over the fowl of the air, and over the cattle, and over all the earth, and over every creeping thing that creepeth upon the earth. So God created man in His own image, in the image of God created He him, male and female created He them. And God blessed them, and God said unto them, Be fruitful, and multiply, and replenish the earth, and subdue it: and have dominion over the fish of the sea, and over the fowl of the air and over every living thing that moveth upon the earth. And God said, Behold, I have given you every herb bearing seed, which is upon the face of all the earth, and every tree, in the which is the fruit of a tree yielding seed; to you it shall be for meat. And to every beast of the earth, and to every fowl of the air, and to every thing that creepeth upon the earth, wherein there is life, I have given every green herb for meat: and it was so, and God saw every thing that He had made, and, behold, it was very good. And the evening and the morning were the sixth day." (Genesis 1: 26-31) We did exist in essence, therefore, but were not yet formed – that is, tested (or stressed, as forced into a mold, or turned by a potter to transform the vessel from his mind to being formed on the wheel) in the world of living things

and created nature.

Then, we were formed, *"And the Lord God formed man of the dust of the ground, and breathed into his nostrils the breath of life; and man became a living soul. And the Lord God planted a garden eastward in Eden; and there He put the man whom He had formed. And out of the ground made the Lord God to grow every tree that is pleasant to the sight, and good for food; the tree of life also in the midst of the garden, and the tree of knowledge of good and evil."* (Genesis 2:7-9) Thus, the fruit of the tree of the knowledge of good and evil, which is to say the experience of both the good (beautiful, gracious, loving, precious, bountiful) and of the evil (adversity, affliction distress, misery) had not yet been 'tasted' by us. The process of our essence was still being transformed into existence among other existences, and on a physical plane.

"And the Lord God took the man, and put him into the garden of Eden to dress it and to keep it. And the Lord God commanded the man, saying, Of every tree of the garden thou mayest freely eat: But of the tree of the knowledge of good and evil, thou shalt not eat of it: for in the day that thou eatest thereof thou shalt surely die. And the Lord God said, It is not good that the man should be alone; I will make him an help meet for him. And out of the ground the Lord God formed every beast of the field, and every fowl of the air; and brought them unto Adam to see what he would call them: and whatsoever Adam called every living creature, that was the name thereof, And Adam gave names to all cattle , and to the fowl of the air, and to every beast of the field; but for Adam there was not found an help meet for him. And the Lord God caused a deep sleep to fall upon Adam, and he slept: and He took one of his ribs, and closed up the flesh instead thereof; And the rib, which the Lord God had taken from man, made He a woman, and brought her unto the man. And Adam said, This is now bone of my bones, and flesh of my flesh: she shall be called Woman, because she was taken out of Man." (Genesis 2:15-23)

Consequently, we came to know evil in the form of opposition or of an adversary, after the 'fall', in the course of things. And sin was to become a matter of 'missing the mark'. And so we were still in the process of 'being formed' or 'molded', but we had not yet 'tasted' hardship, deprivation or adversity. That is, until we ate the apple; and since then, our forming has been on-going. *"And He said, Who told thee that thou wast naked? Hast thou eaten of the tree, whereof I commanded thee that thou shouldest not eat? And the man said, The woman whom Thou gavest to be with me, she gave me of the tree, and I did eat. And the Lord God said unto the woman, What is this that thou hast done? And the woman said, The serpent beguiled me, and I did eat. And the Lord God said unto the serpent, Because thou hast done this, thou art cursed above all cattle, and above every beast of the field; upon thy belly shalt thou go, and dust shalt thou eat all the days of thy life: and I will put enmity between thee and the woman, and between thy seed and her seed; it shall bruise thy head, and thou shalt bruise his heel. Unto the woman He said, I will greatly multiply thy sorrow and thy conception; in sorrow thou shalt bring forth children; and thy desire shall be to thy husband, and he shall rule over thee. And unto Adam He said, Because thou hast hearkened unto the voice of thy wife, and hast eaten of the tree, of which I commanded thee, saying, Thou shalt not eat of it: cursed is the ground for thy sake; in sorrow shalt thou eat of it all the days of thy life; Thorns also and thistles shall it bring forth to thee; and thou shalt eat the herb of the field; In the sweat of thy face shalt thou eat bread, till thou return unto the ground; for out of it was thou taken: for dust thou art, and unto dust shalt thou return. And Adam called his wife's name Eve; because she was the mother of all living."* (Genesis 3:11-20)

Thus, man 'chose' adversity as a lifestyle. This was not God's wish for man, but he disobeyed. Adam now called his mate, Eve, whereas before it was Woman. Further, *"Male and female created He them; and blessed them, and called their name Adam, in the day when they were created."* (Genesis 5:2) Thus, not only two creations but three names for the female?! (1. Adam, the two were one; 2. Woman, from man; 3. Eve, mother of all living.) This adversity and sinning has continued to this day. In carefully reading Genesis 1, 2 and 3 we can imagine the use, perhaps, of an 'evolutionary' type growth of life other than human. For example, *"And God said, Let the waters bring forth abundantly and the moving creature that hath life, and fowl that may fly above the earth in the open firmament of heaven. And God created great whales, and every living creature that moveth, which the waters brought forth abundantly, after their kind, and every winged fowl after its kind: and God saw that it was good. And God blessed them, saying, Be fruitful, and multiply, and fill the waters in the seas, and let fowl multiply in the earth . . ."* (Genesis 1:20-22) *"And out of the ground the Lord God formed every beast of the field, and every fowl of the air . . ."* (Genesis 2:19)

There is even something to be said for God dealing with man in an evolutionary type relationship. (Biblical scholars would use the term 'dispensation'.) From the messages that God gave the prophets and leaders all through the Old Testament, to the Ten Commandments through the dealings with the various kings, culminating in Jesus Christ and His message, His truth, His life and His way. There is so much room for speculation and conjecture – but always, in the final analysis, faith is required. The second creation could represent the transformation from the creation in essence to that of physical existence, in which we fail perfection but must learn that only in God is perfection. Man chose not simply knowledge over life, but immediate physical gratification over faith and immortality. We must become one with God and His WILL – ours.

All the world's woes and human ills are derived from disobedience to God and man exalting himself above God, and this is apparently compounded by the work of Satan, the Accuser and destroyer of humans (and the earth). Satan is often mentioned as the 'prince' of this world (John 12:31, 14:30 and 16:11, 1 Corinthians 2:6 and 2:8.) The devil is also referred to as the 'father' of those Jews who sought to trap or kill Jesus. *"Jesus said unto them, If God were your Father, ye would love me: for I proceeded forth and came from God; neither came I of Myself, but He sent Me. Why do ye not understand My speech? even because ye cannot hear My word. Ye are of your father the devil, and the lusts of your father ye will do. He was a murderer from the beginning, and abode not in the truth, because there is no truth in him. When he speaketh a lie, he speaketh of his own: for he is a liar, and the father of it. And because I tell you the truth, ye believe Me not."* (John 8:42-45)

Further, in this regard, St. Paul called a sorcerer a child of the devil (Acts 13:10). St. John states that, *"He that committeth sin is of the devil; for the devil sinneth from the beginning. For this purpose the Son of God was manifested, that He might destroy the works of the devil."* (1 John 3:8) *"In this the children of God are manifest, and the children of the devil: whosoever doeth not righteousness is not of God, neither he that loveth not his brother."* (1 John 3:10)

The devil was there at our physical beginning, as our destroyer. *"And the great dragon was cast out, that old serpent, called the Devil, and Satan, which deceiveth the whole world: he was cast out into the earth, and his angels were cast out with him."* (Revelation 12:9) *"And he laid hold on the dragon, that old serpent, which is the Devil, and Satan, and bound him a thousand years,"* (Revelation 20:2)

This process of 'forming' us from essence into existence somehow may have introduced sin, that is, the process of transformation from essence into physical existence involving the creation of free choice, and, in the similitude of God, may have involved great risk or a great weeding out, or in some way allowed Satan an opening in order to get to spiritual existence from physical existence. And along the way, God dealt with us in what perhaps might be labeled an 'evolutionary' process. At any rate, first He made Adam – who failed. Then, He had outstanding men such as Noah, Abraham, Isaac, Jacob (Israel), Moses, David, Prophets and Kings – all of whom failed or did not get the job done. During this time, He had a 'people', twelve tribes, a nation and two 'nations', in His plan to have Man be the essence that He created. Finally, after all else had failed, God Himself came to earth through birth and walked on part of His creation as a human being, showing us what He wanted us to be like, in the form of Jesus Christ, Who was, of course, crucified, but gained victory over sin, death and Satan and rose a Spirit of the essence of God's creation – that is, **ACTUAL REALITY**, rather than what we have brought about by our failure, VIRTUAL REALITY. Perhaps God can do no more to rescue us from Satan, death and evil without destroying the essence of the creature having free choice. *"For many are called, but few are chosen."* (Matthew 22:14) Please bear in mind that the foregoing are my speculations and I hope they may at least be profitable in stimulating further thought and interest in the Bible.

One thing that becomes more and more apparent to me is the terrible contagiousness of sin. It spreads quickly and especially from father to sons, and from family to family. God is such a good and loving God, the insidiousness and ubiquitousness of sin is such that it must be dealt with harshly – out of loving concern for the yet innocent or unhardened. The lake of fire may be symbolic in the sense that man is in God's hands as is clay in the potter's, and as long as we are not hardened into sin, we can be reshaped or molded over. But once we love sin and are 'hardened' into it, we are like a clay vessel once it is fired, it is hardened, and if defective, can only be broken, i.e., destroyed.

A quote about Dag Hammarskjold[6], "The transition from despair over himself to faith in God seems to have been a slow process, interrupted by relapses. Two themes came to preoccupy his thoughts. First, the conviction that no man can do properly what he is called upon to do in this life unless he can learn to forget his ego and act as an instrument of God. Second, that for him personally, the way to which he was called would lead to the Cross, i.e., to suffering, worldly humiliation, and the physical sacrifice of his life."

It would appear to be a journey from essence through existence to perfection. *"Therefore, leaving the principles of the doctrine of Christ, let us go on unto perfection; not laying again the foundation of repentance from dead works, and of faith toward God"* (Hebrews 6:1) *"But the God of all grace, Who hath called us unto His eternal glory by Christ Jesus, after that ye have suffered a while, make you perfect, stablish, strengthen, settle you."* (1 Peter 5:10) *"For the perfecting of the saints, for the work of the ministry, for the edifying of the body of Christ."* (Ephesians 4:12)

Chapter 10
Deviltry of Distraction

More and more and more, day after day after day, the people of the major nations appear to have a sybaritic, hedonistic, self-indulgent focus to their lifestyle, behavior and attitude. Get it all now, 'you only live once', me, me, me, 'I'm looking out for number one.' Marriages crumbling, families falling apart, children running their parents, neighborhoods unsafe because of drugs, crime becoming the number one growth industry. Out of Africa comes the HIV virus, which rampages from there throughout the world. Gays and lesbians becoming more politically correct than the religious right. Hate seeping out of the seams of America, even America. American politicians and judiciary losing respect in all quarters of our society where both professionals and tradesmen gouge and cheat the citizen. Juries of regular citizens setting aside truth and justice in favor of prejudice or vengeance. All this on the eve of the 21st century.

There is one voice of sanity and stability, although it is in a choir of discordant other voices. The one voice is that of non-denominational Christianity and it is spread throughout all the denominations and outside of organized religion as well. *"For where two or three are gathered together in My name, there am I in the midst of them."* (Matthew 18:20) The Bible, especially the New Testament, is so filled with wisdom and reality that it truly is he who is blind who cannot see its truths. As the old saying goes, none are so blind as they who will not see.

We are spirits housed within the vehicle of our bodies. It is not because we are so dependent upon our five senses that we have become imprisoned within our bodies, but because we are becoming so increasingly concerned with the gratification of our senses. And this stems from the commercialization of scientific applications which enhance or indulge the senses, for example, stereophonic music, color motion pictures, exotic culinary offerings, taste treats catered to until they become addictive. Alcohol and drugs to jade the chemistry of the brain, fleshly erotic behavior and pornography that becomes not only increasingly perverse but more and more effects the young whose innocent brains are overwhelmed with the sudden, premature in-rushing of a world that panders to basic instincts and are unable to cope with the chemistry unleashed in their confused minds and bodies. Illicit drugs and even alcohol, nicotine and caffeine all send messages to the brain which are incompatible to the body – and the mind must reestablish control. The deprivation of or excessive intake of nutrients (sweets and junk food) puts the body into a state unacceptable to the brain – and the mind must reestablish equilibrium (homeostasis). Unfortunately, the mind is unable to serve this function indefinitely and must be assisted spiritually.

"From whence come wars and fightings among you? come they not hence, even of your lusts that war in your members: Ye lust, and have not: ye kill, and desire to have, and cannot obtain: ye fight and war, yet ye have not, because ye ask not. Ye ask, and receive not, because ye ask amiss, that ye may consume it upon your lusts. Ye adulterers and adulteresses, know ye not that the friendship of the world is enmity with God: whosoever therefore will be a friend of the world is the enemy of God." (James 4:1-4) America honors freedom, but it is endangered by gross personal greed motivated by capitalism, which has become unaccountable and uncontrollable because of the size of the corporations and their increasingly worldwide scope. 'Peace' and 'one world' have become concepts to hoodwink the average citizen, especially as their mind and spirit are more and more numbed by sensuality. The battle cry must go out and it has to be to a **non-violent web of individuals** who are guided by the Holy Spirit of God, and who are both living and proclaiming the way, the truth and the life of Jesus Christ. Nothing else will save even a remnant, but this remnant must exist and grow if freedom is to survive and if the world is to survive. It cannot be violent: anger begets anger as hate begets hate, and both are very, very contagious. It must be a revolution of love kept alive

and possible through hope and Christian faith. *"Ye have heard that it hath been said, Thou shalt love thy neighbour, and hate thine enemy. But I say unto you, Love your enemies, bless them that curse you, do good to them that hate you, and pray for them which despitefully use you, and persecute you; That ye may be the children of your Father which is in heaven: for He maketh His sun to rise on the evil and on the good, and sendeth rain on the just and on the unjust. For if ye love them which love you, what reward have ye: do not even the publicans the same: And if ye salute your brethren only, what do ye more than others: do not even the publicans so: Be ye therefore perfect, even as your Father which is in heaven is perfect."* (Matthew 5:43-48)

Democracy is an attempt to marry freedom and capitalism; however, there is a problem. Capitalistic corporations, as they become bigger (more monopolistic or cartelish), they become bureaucracies just as much as do governments. The basic flaw, however, is the heart of man, the nature of the human; it is not good. At birth, the human mind is not a tabula rasa (a blank slate), it is tarnished, defective and corrupted. Love socializes a baby, hate or neglect bestializes. (If you don't want to think of it in terms of original sin, perhaps you can assuage yourself by thinking in terms of: the 'gene pool'; or even those pseudo-evolutionists can think of it in terms of nature's 'claw and fang' or 'survival of the fittest'). *"Jesus answered and said unto him, Verily, verily, I say unto thee, Except a man be born again, he cannot see the kingdom of God."* (John 3:3) *"For God so loved the world, that He gave His only begotten Son, that whosoever believeth in Him should not perish, but have everlasting life. For God sent not His Son into the world to condemn the world; but that the world through Him might be saved."* (John 3:16-17)

Humor is touted as necessary to be able to get through this vale of tears, that it is invaluable to be able to laugh at oneself. I have no doubt and, in fact, personal experience to attest to this; however, when one is on a mission of gravest consequences, it is even more vital to be focused and dedicated to the objective, especially if it is a life and death matter. Thus, what would one expect if it were a matter between a joyful immortality and a bitter mortality, and indeed, we find throughout the New Testament few, if any, references to fun or humor. There is nothing capricious or impulsive about Christ, nor is there ever anything incongruous or ludicrous or illogical about Him or His behavior. It is time we realized, along with Henry Wadsworth Longfellow that, 'Life is real! Life is earnest! And the grave is not its goal; "Dust thou art, to dust returnest" Was not spoken of the soul.'

It is so important to be disciplined and not to be distracted or preoccupied with all the forms of entertainment, not only available, but 'pushed' upon the average person incessantly. If we allow the intrusion of television, radio, fiction and sports to fix our attention, then our energy and purpose become scattered and unproductive. Of course, there is a place in our daily lives for humor and fun, but not to the extent that it has become over the past fifty years. Too frequently people do not want to take responsibility for their actions, but instead 'project' the 'blame' onto others. People are more and more reluctant to make decisions. *"Submit yourselves therefore to God. Resist the devil, and he will flee from you, Draw nigh to God, and He will draw nigh to you. Cleanse your hands , ye sinners; and purify your hearts, ye double minded. Be afflicted, and mourn, and weep: let your laughter be turned to mourning, and your joy to heaviness. Humble yourselves in the sight of the Lord, and He shall lift you up."* (James 4:7-10)

We need to take things a day at a time, and ourselves – not too seriously. *"Take therefore no thought for the morrow: for the morrow shall take thought for the things of itself. Sufficient unto the day is the evil thereof."* (Matthew 6:34) This world (counterfeit and time-bound) may be Satan's realm (the prince of this world), but Jesus was the supreme representative of God (His only begotten Son), and He shows us the life that overcomes all evil and that is a life of love. *"Now is the judgment of this world: now shall the prince of this world be cast out."* (John 12:31) *"Forasmuch then as the children are partakers of flesh and blood, He also Himself likewise took part of the same; that through death He might destroy him that had the power of death, that is, the devil; And deliver them who through fear of death were all their lifetime subject to bondage."* (Hebrews 2:14-15) *"For none of us liveth to himself, and no man dieth to himself. For whether we live, we live unto the Lord; and whether we die, we die unto the Lord: whether we live therefore, or die, we are the Lord's. For to this end Christ both died, and rose, and revived, that He might be Lord both of the dead and living."* (Romans 14:7-9)

Our God came and participated in and lived in a part of His own creation in our VIRTUAL REALITY. If you have become conversant with computer games or design, and you understand what VIRTUAL REALITY is (see pages 100 and 154), perhaps you can imagine God (Jesus Christ) inserting Himself into our physical world of VIRTAUL REALITY, showing us the way to His **ACTUAL REALITY**. He contrasted our life of virtuality with real Actuality obtainable by us through Christ. He enabled us to see (if we want to) how false, failed, futile and final it is to focus on the present world and human achievements and acquisition to the exclusion of His **ACTUAL REALITY** of love, eternal life and all of the marvelous, fulfilling fruits of the Spirit. This world and its human population, for the most part, is still intrigued, mislead and distracted by the fruit of the 'forbidden apple'.

Today, there is so much form and so little content in all facets of life, extending even to the Presidency. As McDonald states in his book, *The American Presidency*[12], ". . . Hence, it is not enough merely to govern well; the president must also seem presidential. He must inspire confidence in his integrity, compassion, competence, and capacity to take charge in any conceivable situation. . . And he [Clinton] won because he was skillful at projecting an image." (p. 424, 458). In this respect, America has to be increasingly careful not to put too much reliance on campaign oratory and promises; promises often belie the subsequent behavior. Christianity has, for decades, been placed in a position false to the intent of our founding fathers. Freedom from religion in state matters has been preached instead of freedom of religion. Western Christianity has lost its voice and its vote in our democracy, even though it was one of the basic foundation stones at its inception and establishment. The way Evans sums up much of what he writes in his excellent book, *The Theme is Freedom*[3], "... Recovery of our religious faith and its teachings should be our first and main concern. Without it, nothing much by way of practical improvement can be accomplished. With it, all the rest might readily be added." (p. 323) This type of writing appears to be a sign of the times, especially when common sense and religious values are appearing on our scene in 1996 America in many areas of life to an increasing degree. There is a growing tendency to compare present day American lifestyles and loss of basic values with that of Rome in its days of decline.

Freedom is so helpful in our individual efforts to find Christ and to live as we believe He wants. But our democracy and its freedom have been jeopardized over the past half century, outlined succinctly by Hayek in *The Road to Serfdom*[7]. In discussing the conflict between the 'security' of being taken care of by the state (which eventuates in dictatorship) and the risk of individual effort and independence, i.e. between socialism (which he equates with liberals of the last fifty years) and free enterprise, he states, "Either both the choice and the risk rest with the individual or he is relieved of both." (p. 140) To become a Christian takes the ultimate in risk and is a difficult choice, but I don't believe nearly as risky or difficult in a free America as in a dictatorship. So it behooves Christians to exercise their right to vote, to keep informed and to keep legislators apprised of their wishes. We are in the world but not of the world. *"I pray not that Thou shouldest take them out of the world, but that thou shouldest keep them from the evil. They are not of the world, even as I am not of the world."* (John 17:15-16)

Finally, it seems to me that somehow competition and rivalry have gotten out of control in our capitalistic democracy. It is not Christian, it is ruthless; and in America, success and acceptance is measured in terms of dollars amassed whether by corporations or individuals. There needs to be some limit set on personal incomes; after all, the satisfaction of the job should count for something, as well as should the sense of contributing to the society. Honor should not go to the greatest bilkers. Why must we go to such extremes that we have starving babies, seniors and handicapped people while some have three or four palatial homes, jet planes, millions even billions in the bank? It would compensate to some degree if, in later years, they are philanthropic; if the philanthropy reflects a growing wisdom and a change of heart, rather than further self-aggrandizement. After all, we all are in need of forgiveness. This evil must be moderated and we don't have to throw out the baby with the bathwater. Democracy and capitalism have their place, and they are far superior to dictatorships and communism/socialism. However, without conversion to Christianity by our leaders in all walks of life, I do not foresee the correction of this flaw as it stems from the human heart. This does not bode well for the future. The story of Lazarus is appropriate here.

"There was a certain rich man, which was clothed in purple and fine linen, and fared sumptuously every day: And there was a certain beggar named Lazarus, which was laid at his gate, full of sores, And desiring to be fed with the crumbs which fell from the rich man's table: moreover the dogs came and licked his sores. And it came to pass, that beggar died, and was carried by the angels into Abraham's bosom: the rich man also died, and was buried; And in hell he lift up his eyes, being in torments, and seeth Abraham afar off, and Lazarus in his bosom. And he cried and said, Father Abraham, have mercy on me, and send Lazarus, that he may dip the tip of his finger in water, and cool my tongue; for I am tormented in this flame. But Abraham said, Son, remember that thou in thy lifetime receivedst thy good things, and likewise Lazarus evil things: but now he is comforted, and thou art tormented. And beside all this, between us and you there is a great gulf fixed: so that they which would pass from hence to you cannot; neither can they pass to us, that would come from thence. Then he said, I pray thee therefore, father, that thou wouldest send him to my father's

house: For I have five brethren; that he may testify unto them, lest they also come into this place of torment. Abraham saith unto him, They have Moses and the prophets; let them hear them. And he said, Nay, father Abraham: but if one went unto them from the dead, they will repent. And he said unto him, If they hear not Moses and the prophets, neither will they be persuaded, though one rose from the dead." (Luke 16:19-31)

Yes, this is serious business, this business of living, and there is meaning to our individual lives. A growing number of adults 'play' more than their children. Humans, in general, seek entertainment more and more of the time, becoming bored quickly, ironically with more attention to distractions becoming more distractible – from the distractions! This no longer applies just to books, television entertainment, games, new purchases of adult 'toys', food, but increasingly to marriage, family and other committed relationships when they aren't fun (romantic) anymore – too bad for the children. But who really cares? To transfer from artificiality and counterfeit living (Virtuality) requires beseeching God through Jesus Christ, devotion, dedication and effort in order to ever partake in immortality (Actuality). The devil isn't in the details, he is in the distractions. He probably would like us to become clones of him, but it serves his purpose if we merely become puppets, with the strings often being 'pulled' by the media, who in turn are usually controlled by: huge industries (entertainment, manufacturing, health, commerce) or by minds set and closed with some 'vested idealism', i.e., self-serving interest.

From the Spring 1995 issue of *Time* titled, "Welcome to Cyberspace", by Philip Elmer–DeWitt, "It started as the big ideas in technology often do, with a science fiction writer, William Gibson, a young expatriate American living in Canada, was wandering past the video arcades on Vancouver's Granville Street in the early 1980's when something about the way the players were hunched over their glowing screens struck him as odd. 'I could see in the physical intensity of their postures how rapt the kids were,' he says. 'It was like a feedback loop, with photons coming off the screens into the kids' eyes, neurons moving through their bodies and electrons moving through the video games. These kids clearly believed in the space games projected.'" (p. 4) *"Neither be ye idolaters, as were some of them; as it is written, The people sat down to eat and drink, and rose up to play."* (1 Corinthians 10:7) *"Let us walk honestly, as in the day; not in rioting and drunkenness, not in chambering and wantonness, not in strife and envying. But put ye on the Lord Jesus Christ, and make not provision for the flesh, to fulfill the lusts thereof."* (Romans 13:13-14)

Chapter 11
Being Called a Believer or Being Chosen a Saint

Almighty God walked this earth as Jesus Christ and, after the resurrection of The Lord, He sent His Holy Spirit to be with those of us whom He has called and who have chosen to be led by Him. Think of it. The only God Who exists, The Creator of all that exists in any manner or form, substance or activity, essence or existence; has chosen to perfect and make immortal those of us who wish to obey, please, serve and worship Him. Only He can open our eyes and ears to the truth, only He can reveal how Satan tries to confuse and defeat us, and only He can deliver us from sin, Satan and the prison of our carnal minds, through Jesus Christ Who is the Way and the Truth and the Life. We must take up our cross, deny ourselves, and follow Him, which is possible only with the help of the Holy Spirit. Therefore, if you desire to read the Bible, or if it makes sense to you, or if you are seeking out a Biblical pastor or teacher, this means you have been called because only God can open your eyes and your ears to the truth and deliver you from the spell of Satan. Then, it is up to you to work to be chosen through prayer, study and seeking spiritual empowerment and guidance to free yourself from Satan and your own carnal nature. Demonstrate this in your life by manifesting the gifts of the Spirit toward your fellow man (all men), the essence of which is love. We deserve it not, we earn it not; this calling and growth of faith is all a gift through the grace of God. It is verified, to ourselves and others by our life, i.e., our walk and our works.

In today's idiom, we talk the talk and walk the walk, which is only possible through the Holy Spirit. I believe that it is a growth process, and that is why faith and hope are so basic and vital. We cannot match power or wits with the devil and we must come to Christ as babies and yet become, as Jesus says, *"Behold, I send you forth as sheep in the midst of wolves: be ye therefore wise as serpents, and harmless as doves."* (Matthew 10:16) Some of us have our eyes and ears opened up to the futility of this world and the awareness of a titanic cosmic struggle between God and Satan involving man at a young age, some at an advanced age, and others struggle with doubt and self for decades before resolving it finally for good or evil. But choose we must, and as we choose so we are chosen.

It is absolutely imperative that we understand what is meant by our choosing. It is not like choosing an answer to a multiple choice question, nor is it like choosing where to go on vacation this year. It is a life and death decision, one that involves your lifestyle, one that requires making constant decisions the rest of your life. In other words, it is a decision that becomes an ongoing process of decision making (and of course no decision is a decision). At this time, my personal feeling is that when one tries turning constantly to the Holy Ghost for guidance, as well as striving to turn one's life over to Jesus Christ as 'the way, the truth and the life', and allows the love of God to be shed in one's heart and shed abroad to others, then one would have become what I have designated elsewhere (pages 62-63 and 66) as a saint and who would be resurrected without any fear of experiencing the second death.

On the other hand, I would think that being simply a believer, still making wrong choices or decisions mixed in with right choices and decisions, the situation would be different at the end when the books are opened. One would be judged on an overall basis of one's life, and that would determine to what degree one would be exposed to the danger of the second death and the lake of fire, as in, *"If any man's work shall be burned, he shall suffer loss: but he himself shall be saved; yet so as by fire."* (1 Corinthians 3:15)

This matter of how you live and who or what you worship is of the ultimate importance; there is nothing more important. So if you are one whose eyes and ears are open, just realize that you are one of the, *"Multitudes, multitudes in the valley of decision: for the day of the Lord is near in the valley of decision."* (Joel 3:14), know this (to quote John Donne), that it is you "for whom the bell tolls" and that you have been 'called', but that being chosen will be on the basis of your ongoing decisions and only upon your decisions, (that is, to what degree God is at the center of your life, behavior and thoughts). It is scary, but you are in the hands of the Living God Who has provided you with His Holy Spirit, and that this has been made possible through the life and sacrifice of the Lord Jesus Christ; faith is a precious gift given to you but with grave responsibilities and consequences. *"So the last shall be first, and the first last: for many be called, but few chosen."* (Matthew 20:16) Faith, hope and love must become categorical imperatives for you. *"Therefore being justified by faith, we have peace with God through our Lord Jesus Christ: By Whom also we have access by faith into this grace wherein we stand, and rejoice in hope of the glory of God. And not only so, but we glory in tribulations also: knowing that tribulation worketh patience; And patience, experience; and experience, hope: And hope maketh not ashamed; because the love of God is shed abroad in our hearts by the Holy Ghost which is given unto us."* (Romans 5:1-5)

"For to be carnally minded is death; but to be spiritually minded is life and peace. Because the carnal mind is enmity against God: for it is not subject to the law of God, neither indeed can be. So then they that are in the flesh cannot please God." (Romans 8:6-8) So, if you are centered in the self and in this world, then God is outside of your frame of reference when you 'pray' to Him for carnal things, because your carnal (natural, worldly, sensuous, temporal, fleshly, animal) mind is at enmity with God. It remains so until your eyes and ears are 'opened' and you begin to seek God and seek to become spiritually minded. *"Ye ask, and receive not, because ye ask amiss, that ye may consume it upon your lusts."* (James 4:3) Further, *"But the natural man receiveth not the things of the Spirit of God: for they are foolishness unto him: neither can he know them, because they are spiritually discerned."* (1 Corinthians 2:14)

In case you are plagued with doubts about God and/or yourself, take heart, because the ongoing battle centers around faith and overcoming doubt – which constantly encroaches. *"For we are saved by hope: but hope that is seen is not hope: for what a man seeth, why doth he yet hope for? But if we hope for that we see not, then do we with patience wait for it."* (Romans 8:24-25) If you have not already been doing it, I would strongly recommend that whenever a Biblical reference or quotation interests you or provokes your curiosity – look it up and read further in that context. Although I quote from the King James Version, you might wish to use the New King James Version for more clarity of language.

"And I, brethren, could not speak unto you as unto spiritual, but as unto carnal, even as unto babes in Christ. I have fed you with milk, and not with meat: for hitherto ye were not able to bear it, neither yet now are ye able. For ye are yet carnal: for whereas there is among you envying, and strife, and divisions, are ye not carnal, and walk as men?" (1 Corinthians 3:1-3) (See also Hebrews 5:11-13.) Salvation is a growth process.

Faith and being called is a gift from God, it is unearned and undeserved. *"So then it is not of him that willeth, nor of him that runneth, but of God that sheweth mercy."* (Romans 9:16) *"For they being ignorant of God's righteousness, and going about to establish their own righteousness, have not submitted themselves unto the righteousness of God. For Christ is the end of the law for righteousness to every one that believeth."* (Romans 10:3-4) *"That if thou shalt confess with thy mouth the Lord Jesus, and shalt believe in thine heart that God hath raised Him from the dead, Thou shalt be saved."* (Romans 10:9) *"And be not conformed to this world: but be ye transformed by the renewing of your mind, that ye may prove what is that good, and acceptable, and perfect, will of God."* (Romans 12:2) *"For whatsoever things were written aforetime were written for our learning, that we through patience and comfort of the scriptures might have hope."* (Romans 15:4) *"Now the God of hope fill you with all joy and peace in believing, that ye may abound in hope, through the power of the Holy Ghost."* (Romans 15:13) *"For after that in the wisdom of God the world by wisdom knew not God, it pleased God by the foolishness of preaching to save them that believe. For the Jews require a sign, and the Greeks seek after wisdom: But we preach Christ crucified, unto the Jews a stumbling block, and unto the Greeks foolishness: But unto them which are called, both Jews and Greeks, Christ the power of God, and the wisdom of God. Because the foolishness of God is wiser than men; and the weakness of God is stronger than men. For ye see your calling brethren, how that not many wise men after the flesh, not many mighty, not many noble, are called: And base things of the world, and things which are despised, hath God chosen, yea, and things which are not, to bring to nought things that are: That no flesh should glory in His presence. But of Him are ye in Christ Jesus who of God is made unto us wisdom, and righteousness, and sanctification, and redemption: That, as according as it is written, He that glorieth, let him glory in the Lord."* (1 Corinthians 1:21-31)

How hard it is for someone who is rich or powerful or even moderately successful to turn to God and really seek guidance from the Holy Spirit and true reformation of his life. It is so easy to be compromised by our ego, our friends, our goals or our lifestyle. It comes home to us why the Lord said: *"Hearken, my beloved brethren, Hath not God chosen the poor of this world rich in faith, and heirs of the kingdom which He hath promised to them that love Him?"* (James 2:5)

This book is not about 'proving' the Bible. God requires faith; therefore, God and the Bible are not provable. You need the Bible in order to know about God, Jesus Christ and the Holy Ghost and how to relate to Them and to find out what They require of you. Since faith is a gift from God, it is vital to make an effort to find out whether you have been gifted with faith through the grace of God, if you do not already know it. If you are concerned and seeking faith and you have read this far, assume you do have faith. So the 'battle' is joined because Satan does not want you to have a working, living faith in Jesus Christ and God. Doubt, disbelief and distrust in God are major ways he attempts to break down faith, an auxiliary method is to cause doubt as to whether we have faith or are even redeemable.

We must live in our faith, that is, in God or by the directing of the Holy Ghost and not by our heart because, *"The heart is deceitful above all things, And desperately wicked; Who can know it? I, the Lord, search the heart, I test the mind, Even to give every man according to his ways, According to the fruit of his doings."* (Jeremiah 17:9-10) So, through our faith, we give our heart over to God and, ever since Genesis, God has been remaking men as they submit and give themselves to Him. *"The word which came to Jeremiah from the Lord, saying: 'Arise and go down to the potter's house, and there I will cause you to hear My words.' Then I went down to the potter's house, and there he was, making something at the wheel. And the vessel that he made of clay was marred in the hand of the potter; so he made it again into another vessel, as it seemed good to the potter to make, Then the word of the Lord came to me, saying; 'O house of Israel, can I not do with you as this potter?' says the Lord. 'Look, as the clay is in the potter's hand, so are you in My hand, O house of Israel!'"* (Jeremiah 18:1-6)

So it must be, so it has to be, so it will be, if you want to love God *"with all your heart, and with all your soul, and with all your mind"* as Jesus said to do and to *"love your neighbor as yourself"* (Matthew 22:37, 22:39). As St. Paul said, *"Not that I speak in respect of want: for I have learned, in whatsoever state I am, therewith to be content. I know both how to be abased, and I know how to abound: everywhere and in all things I am instructed both to be full and to be hungry, both to abound and to suffer need. I can do all things through Christ which strengtheneth me."* (Philippians 4:11-13) Jesus was God in our world showing us the way, giving us hope, establishing our faith and showing us the life that overcomes all evil, that is, the life of love.

This is, of course, my interpretation, but it seems to me that the difference between a saint and a believer is the degree of dedication to 'making yourself a workman of God' and being constantly guided by the Holy Ghost, instead of intermittently. However, I do believe that it is crucial to be really committed to Jesus Christ and to grow in the sense of the presence and love of God. In neither case, saint or believer, is 'lukewarm' acceptable. *"So then because thou art lukewarm, and neither cold nor hot, I will spue thee out of My mouth."* (Revelation 3:16) *"No man can serve two masters; for either he will hate the one, and love the other; or else he will hold to the one and despise the other. Ye cannot serve God and mammon."* (Matthew 6:24)

Chapter 12
Cruelty of Competition

This chapter is about America, specifically the United States, where we are unconsciously trying to prove Darwinism through capitalistic democracy. Success is the ultimate here, where possessing money not only brings power but adulation as well, even if it is through prostitution and drugs, or through 'genius' combining invention with production, such as running a company that manufactures cars or establishes a network of communication. Our 'heroes' apparently include the Al Capones, the Marylin Monroes, or the rock and porn stars, or the robber barons; as well as the Henry Fords and the Thomas Edison's. The 'great' men we idolize include Alexander the Great, Julius Ceasar, Ghengis Khan and Napoleon; these 'great' men had millions of other men slaughtered for their own ambitions and they were masters of intrigue, deceit, betrayal and often encouraged their soldiers to rape, murder, plunder and pillage civilian cities. Certainly, we also praise others on the order of Eisenhower and Churchill, but we call them all our heroes, build monuments to them and encourage emulation. In other words, 'success' means everything; all is sacrificed in the temple of money and/or power at the altar of ego. I am not critical of 'success' per se, and industriousness; hard work and entrepreneurialism are all to be lauded, as is ambition. What is portentous is the degree to which competition and ambition have become increasingly cutthroat without rules or ethics so that these two, competition and ambition, blend into greed and ruthless domination, entirely self-serving, lacking any redeeming features.

Most Americans would find it difficult to name a single man or woman that excites them and that they would want to devote their life to be like, whom the world either ignores or merely pays lip service to when it is politically advantageous. I speak of ones such as Schweitzer, St. Paul, Ghandi, Mother Teresa, etc. Those who can deserve congratulations as they are in the minority; not many of them, however, would continue to shape their lives in such a fashion much beyond the age of twenty-two. Most would admit, if they were being honest, that they might be tempted to do almost anything to be a president of a large corporation, a general or admiral, a stage or screen star, a very successful lawyer or politician. Success in all these stem from severe competition, in other words, survival of the fittest. And that phrase covers a multitude of sins: stepping on other people, lying and other forms of deceit, using people, neglecting or rejecting your loved ones. It is total absorption in self and the goal in which any means are justified by the end. AND, at the end, one is more mortal, more carnal and more dissatisfied than ever before. Look at Howard Hughes, probably our first well known billionaire. His end was bitter, paranoid, self-imposed isolation, sick and alone. Or take Marylin Monroe, who reportedly took her own life, unhappy and allegedly drugged out of reality.

Americans, by and large, are so into denial and self-aggrandizement they cannot see and will not hear. Doesn't it make sense when the Lord says, *"Then said Jesus unto His disciples, Verily I say unto you, That a rich man shall hardly enter into the kingdom of heaven."* (Matthew 19:23) And St. Paul states, *"For ye see your calling, brethren, how that not many wise men after the flesh, not many mighty, not many noble, are called: But God hath chosen the foolish things of the world to confound the wise; and God hath chosen the weak things of the world to confound the things which are mighty; And base things of the world, and things which are despised, hath God chosen, yea, and things which are not, to bring to nought things that are: That no flesh should glory in His presence."* (1 Corinthians 1:26-29)

The nature of competition is partly determined by its goals, as is the nature of corporations or cartels. Here in America, as competition becomes more severe and fierce (as it almost always does in any field of endeavor), it can quickly become cruel and increasingly self-serving and heartless. Power, wealth or domination and perks (perquisites) can become 'the bottom line'; all else is subordinate. This has had a lot to do with the undermining of the family, because so many corporations tend to move its personnel wherever and whenever they choose, uprooting children from schools and neighborhoods, taking fathers away from families, etc. We have become a nation of gypsies with no roots, no history and no future. Divorce becomes rampant and then children have parents or a parent, but in name only. They don't have their presence, their attention or their love. For a corporate executive, there is almost total commitment to the 'firm'; however, that goes if he is betrayed by the company when his 'usefulness' is over or he becomes too burdensome because of the growing fringe benefits and perquisites. The end is one of no loyalties, no families (in any real meaning of the word); it becomes a loveless angry nation of the elite and the dispossessed. The irony is that the 'elite' have nothing as well because the value of life is not in its carnality or possessions, it is in the spiritual values of love and joy and faith.

Where is the commitment to the children? It has become the idolatry to leaders, and the leaders have failed the people because they have failed themselves. Civilization and culture are man's edifices and have a false basis – ego gratification and sensual pleasure, i.e., carnality. A murderer (Cain) was reputedly the founder of the first city – the inhabitants of which were further said to have reached an advanced stage of civilization with proficiency in music and the arts.[5, 15]

The goals, the ends, the means, the process must become love and that cannot come about by man's efforts, because Satan is opposed and man must choose God Who alone is victorious as established by Jesus Christ. Only through Him and the Holy Spirit can humans break out of their VIRTUAL REALITY into His **ACTUAL REALITY** of love and immortality.

In God's process of creation, He created the idea (the essence), then the structure (existence), and then the function (perfection); and this process, at least in this world, involves good versus evil, with good eventually triumphant and eternal. Humans go from selfishness and self-seeking (VIRTUAL REALITY) to selflessness in which resides peace, joy and love, with hope and faith being replaced by the **ACTUAL REALITY** of God's presence and our oneness with Him. But we cannot understand the import of the foregoing; it is alien to us and unacceptable to most. We assume that we lose our identity. We don't – we retain our individuality and uniqueness, I believe. I do not think words can express nor images portray what it means to be one with God. In some ways, I think it is an abandonment of self-centeredness, self-consciousness, and self-seeking, and a replacment by a oneness with, a belonging to, and having a wonderfully heightened awareness of BEING – in the presence of Almighty God.

In the meantime, it would be time well spent to study the mind of St. Paul displayed throughout all his letters to the Romans, Corinthians, Galatians, Ephesians, Philippians, Colossians, Thessalonians, Timothy, Titus, Philemon and Hebrews (authorship by Paul is not certain). As well as studying the heart of St. John in the Gospel according to John, and the first, second and third letters of John (there is some dispute about the authorship of the first letter of John, but if he was not the author, then whoever wrote it incorporated a great deal of John's previous thoughts and writings). Revelation may be better left to later on unless you are a student of the Bible.

Above all, however, put what you learn into practice in your life. Read prayerfully and wait on the Holy Spirit whenever a passage confuses you. You will receive guidance and you will be able to absorb it and make it real in your life – eventually. Patience is part of faith.

Civilization, culture and society are all oriented toward and based upon pride, power and pleasure. Most of the elite, the families (if not the founders) of the wealthy, the famous and the powerful, appear to live by the pleasure principle and view life at its best when partying or playing. This world has become a playground for the devil and all the actors are but pawns in bringing about their own demise. Conceivably, even war is satisfying for the bomb makers and sometimes war seems to be dished up as entertainment for television viewers. The public's thirst for escape from the humdrum makes them a 'market' for bad news, spicy gossip and other sleaze. The common man increasingly aspires to be like the rich and famous who, according to Robin Leach, think the best thing about having money is to show the world they have it, with yachts, parties, mansions, 'charities', extravaganzas and revelry.

There is no substance to any of it; it is all worldly and merely pays lip service to God and to qualities such as love and faith. *"There is no man that hath power over the spirit to retain the spirit; neither hath he power in the day of death: and there is no discharge in that war; neither shall wickedness deliver those that are given to it."* (Ecclesiastes 8:8) *"Because the sentence against an evil work is not executed speedily, therefore the heart of the sons of men is fully set in them to do evil."* (Ecclesiastes 8:11) This does not mean that we have to renounce all and go live in a cave; it does mean that mankind got off on the wrong foot from the beginning. Man continued on the same path of pride and willfulness, which brought about the great flood with only Noah and his family surviving. Tragically, Noah fell short, as did one of his three sons and later generations of the other two sons as well, which eventually led to the tower of Babel. This downward spiritual movement did not stop with the tower of Babel. Man continues to err to this day.

"Let every man abide in the same calling wherein he was called." (1 Corinthians 7:20) Each one of us must continue to live in the world and provide for our family. If we live in a Christian community, then it is much easier to raise children but, if not, then we must continue to function in our communities. We are aliens in a strange land, spiritual beings whose time (and place) has not come and we live among a society of carnal, temporal beings. *"I pray not that Thou shouldest take them out of the world, but that Thou shouldest keep them from the evil. They are not of the world, even as I am not of the world. Sanctify them through Thy truth: As Thou hast sent Me into the world, even so have I also sent them into the world."* (John 17:15-18)

"Because it is written, Be ye holy; for I am holy. And if ye call on the Father, Who without respect of persons judgeth according

to every man's work, pass the time of your sojourning here in fear: Forasmuch as ye know that ye were not redeemed with corruptible things, as silver and gold, from your vain conversation received by tradition from your fathers; But with the precious blood of Christ, as of a lamb without blemish and without spot: Who verily was foreordained before the foundation of the world, but was manifest in these last times for you, who by Him do believe in God, that raised Him up from the dead, and gave Him glory; that your faith and hope might be in God." (1 Peter 1:16-21)

The 'tradition from your fathers' points out the flaw that men's ways are passed down generation to generation, and sin, such as pride, hate, greed and lust, spread like wildfire. They are extremely contagious. Yet today, we hardly give it a second thought to expose our children to all the pornography and violence rampant in the movies, on the television and rife in our music. *"Now therefore ye are no more strangers and foreigners, but fellow citizens with the saints, and of the household of God; And are built upon the foundation of the apostles and prophets, Jesus Christ Himself being the chief corner stone; In Whom all the building fitly framed together groweth unto an holy temple in the Lord: In whom ye also are builded together for an habitation of God through the Spirit."* (Ephesians 2:19-22)

So through the Holy Spirit, living true to our faith, we may not only be spared the end of carnal humans and reap the reward of spirituality and immortality in oneness with Almighty God and Jesus Christ; but perhaps through us God will reach and convert other humans from carnality to spirituality. *"Dearly beloved, I beseech you as strangers and pilgrims, abstain from fleshly lusts, which war against the soul; Having your conversation honest among the Gentiles; that, whereas they speak against you as evildoers, they may by your good works, which they shall behold, glorify God in the day of visitation."* (1 Peter 2:11-12) We are to obey authorities, we are, so to speak, living in their house and they set the rules.

"Submit yourselves to every ordinance of man for the Lord's sake: whether it be to the king, as supreme; Or unto governors, as

unto them that are sent by him for the punishment of evildoers, and for the praise of them that do well. For so is the will of God, that with well doing ye may put to silence the ignorance of foolish men: As free, and not using your liberty for a cloak of maliciousness, but as the servants of God. Honour all men, Love the brotherhood, Fear God. Honour the king." (1 Peter 2:13-17) We are to be law-abiding, good citizens, not insurrectionists; ego fulfillment is diametrically opposed to Christianity. In fact, competition and rivalry are basic human characteristics, which, along with disobedience (being a law unto one's self), have resulted in man's difficulties. Chief among the so-called accomplishments of competition have been cities, cultures, ethnicities, and 'luxuries'; all of which have rooted and grounded us in the delusion of the carnal and have fostered the belief in the creed of the 'survival of the fittest', blinding most of mankind to God and making this physical world and man's achievements as the be-all and end-all. We are to do all with love, the accomplishments of which would so far exceed rivalry and competition that, in fact, we would have a utopian world, here on earth instead of a war-torn and worn-out world.

It may be argued by some that competition can be healthy, fun and fruitful, promoting Christian growth, both in humans and in organizations. But if that is true, it has to be within not only fair and honest confines, but under the guidance of individual or group inspiration by the Holy Ghost, and not for personal gain of worldly goods or domination. Fierce human competition, where 'worldly ends' are sought and 'justifying' any means, is evil. The cruelty of competition derives from the attitude that all is fair in competition. Competition must be done in the spirit of Christian love, otherwise, it is cruel. The words compete and competition are not even in the Bible – anywhere. Competition implies strife, rivalry and contention, and the very word is from the Roman empire. (Websters Third New International Dictionary, unabridged, defines competitor as, 1a: 'one that seeks what another seeks or claims what another claims'.) Yet, in this modern age, 'competition' is everything when it is followed by success (which in effect means acquisition and/or domination). *"Let nothing be done through strife or vain-glory; but in lowliness of mind let each esteem other better than themselves."* (Philippians 2:3)

Chapter 13
The Still Small Voice

There are favorite passages in the Bible that I call upon at different times, and they provide me with comfort, peace, strength or whatever my particular need is. I repeat them to myself and it is a form of prayer calling upon God to make that particular word or thought operative within me. This has been most helpful to me, and perhaps if you do not already use this type of communication with the Lord or the Comforter, you may find it to be very helpful as well. We humans are flawed and yet we are by no means rejected by our Creator. The entire Bible shows in how many ways and at how many times God is constantly reaching out to us. He loves us, and once we become even dimly aware of this, experientially, we are in a position to respond to Him and 'feel' His presence in everything, everywhere – where we are concerned. He makes Himself known in the little mundane things of everyday life, not just on the special occasions or victories, defeats or crises. He wants you and He wants you to 'experience' Him increasingly. He is with you every instant and when He communicates with you, it is usually with 'a still small voice', but a voice without words or sound. It is a Presence that sometimes you feel and sometimes you just 'know'; but it is, in my experience, a 'kenning'. For faith and hope are still required, as God's communication in these times is not 'provable' or often physically demonstrated, thus you always have to be on guard against doubt. What follows are the most frequently used passages and under some of the circumstances I might use them.

In bed at night, if I can't calm down and go to sleep, perhaps because I am excited in a positive way about some things I plan to do the next day, or maybe I am worried or anxious about problems coming up. In these situations, the following passages are very helpful to repeat, think about, visualize or dwell upon in a supplicating way:

"Be still, and know that I am God. . ." (Psalm 46:10)

"*. . . Peace, be still. . .*" (Mark 4:39)

"*Take therefore no thought for the morrow: for the morrow shall take thought for the things of itself. Sufficient unto the day is the evil thereof.*" (Matthew 6:34)

"*For by grace are ye saved through faith: and that not of yourselves: it is the gift of God: Not of works, lest any man should boast.*" (Ephesians 2:8-9)

"*And ye shall know the truth, and the truth shall make you free.*" (John 8:32)

At times when I am fearful:

"*There is no fear in love; but perfect love casteth out fear: because fear hath torment. He that feareth is not made perfect in love.*" (1 John 4:18)

"*And the peace of God, which passeth all understanding, shall keep your hearts and minds through Christ Jesus.*" (Philippians 4:7)

"*Peace I leave with you, My peace I give unto you: not as the world giveth, give I unto you, Let not your heart be troubled, neither let it be afraid.*" (John 14:27)

"*For God hath not given us the spirit of fear; but of power, and of love, and of a sound mind.*" (2 Timothy 1:7)

"*Who shall separate us from the love of Christ? Shall tribulation, or distress, or persecution, or famine, or nakedness, or peril, or sword? As it is written, For thy sake we are killed all the day long; we are accounted as sheep for the slaughter. Nay, in all these things we are more than conquerors through Him that loved us. For I am persuaded, that neither death, nor life, nor angels, nor principalities, nor powers, nor things present, nor things to come, Nor height, nor depth, nor any other creature, shall be able to separate us from the love of God, which is in Christ Jesus our Lord.*" (Romans 8:35-39)

When I am hurting physically or feeling weak or insecure:

"*And He said unto me, My grace is sufficient for thee: for My strength is made perfect in weakness. . ."* (2 Corinthians 12:9)

"I can do all things through Christ which strengtheneth me." (Philippians 4:13)

"And He said, Go Forth, and stand upon the mount before the Lord, And behold, the Lord passed by, and a great and strong wind rent the mountains, and brake in pieces the rocks before the Lord; but the Lord was not in the earthquake; And after the earthquake a fire; but the Lord was not in the fire: and after the fire a still small voice; And it was so, when Elijah heard it, that he wrapped his face in his mantle, and went out, and stood in the entering in of the cave. And, behold, there came a voice unto him, and said, What doest thou here, Elijah?" (1 Kings 19:11-13)

When I have met misfortune or some disappointment:

"And we know that all things work together for good to them that love God, to them who are the called according to His purpose." (Romans 8:28) [N.B. called, not just the chosen.]

"Then he answered and spake unto me, saying, This is the word of the Lord unto Zerubbabel, saying, Not by might, nor by power, but by My Spirit, saith the Lord of hosts." (Zechariah 4:6)

"Ask, and it shall be given you; seek, and ye shall find; knock, and it shall be opened unto you: For every one that asketh receiveth; and he that seeketh findeth; and to him that knocketh it shall be opened." (Matthew 7:7-8)

When I feel confrontational or irritated or angry:

"But love ye your enemies, and do good, and lend, hoping for nothing again; and your reward shall be great, and ye shall be the children of the Highest: for He is kind unto the unthankful and to the evil." (Luke 6:35)

"For it is God which worketh in you both to will and to do of His good pleasure. Do all things without murmurings and disputings: That ye may be blameless and harmless, the sons of God, without rebuke, in the midst of a crooked and perverse nation, among whom ye shine as lights in the world." (Philippians 2:13-14)

"For he that will love life, and see good days, let him refrain his tongue from evil, and his lips that they speak no guile: Let him eschew evil, and do good; let him seek peace, and ensue it." (1 Peter 3:10-11)

And when my faith is at low ebb or I fear that I don't have the Spirit of God within, even that perhaps I am beyond redemption!

"But whoso keepeth His word, in him verily is the love of God perfected: hereby know we that we are in Him. He that saith he abideth in Him ought himself also so to walk, even as He walked." (1 John 2:5-6)

"Beloved, let us love one another: for love is of God; and every one that loveth is born of God, and knoweth God. He that loveth not knoweth not God; for God is love." (1 John 4:7-8)

"For we are saved by hope: but hope that is seen is not hope: for what a man seeth, why doth he yet hope for? But if we hope for that we see not, then do we with patience wait for it." (Romans 8:24-25)

"And not only so, but we glory in tribulations also: knowing that tribulation worketh patience; And patience, experience; and experience, hope: And hope maketh not ashamed; because the love of God is shed abroad in our hearts by the Holy Ghost which is given unto us." (Romans 5:3-5)

"Neither shall they say, Lo here! or, lo there! for, behold, the kingdom of God is within you." (Luke 17:21)

When I need to remind myself that I am already redeemed by Christ and that when I do or say or think something sinful, that it isn't me, it is sin in me, which I reject, in my growth toward being spiritually minded. At these times, it is strengthening in the battle against the wiles of Satan to read the following passages of St. Paul in his letter to the Romans:

"For we know that the law is spiritual: but I am carnal, sold under sin. For that which I do I allow not: for what I would, that do I not; but what I hate, that do I. If then, I do that which I would

not, I consent unto the law that it is good. Now then it is no more I that do it, but sin that dwelleth in me; For I know that in me (that is, in my flesh), dwelleth no good thing: for to will is present with me; but how to perform that which is good, I find not. For the good that I would I do not: but the evil which I would not, that I do. Now if I do that I would not, it is no more I that do it, but sin that dwelleth in me. I find then a law, that, when I would do good, evil is present with me. For I delight in the law of God after the inward man: But I see another law in my members, warring against the law of my mind, and bringing me into captivity to the law of sin which is in my members. O wretched man that I am! who shall deliver me from the body of this death? I thank God through Jesus Christ our Lord. So then with the mind I myself serve the law of God; but with the flesh the law of sin." (Romans 7:14-25)

Meditating on how much I treasure the gifts that God gives and how much more I want them than riches, power, things or sensuous states:

"But the fruit of the Spirit is love, joy, peace, longsuffering, gentleness, goodness, faith, Meekness, temperance: against such there is no law." (Galatians 5:22-23)

When I am inclined to have doubts about the futility of civilization and consider mankind to have made 'progress'. If I begin thinking that man has, after all, built a pretty good social order and that the Bible is too hard on the achievements of man, then I begin to gloss over the atrocities and injustices going on continuously all over the world. These doubts about the Bible's representations of man's world usually tend to come when everything is fine in my life, and I am not reading the Bible or praying enough, not keeping the presence of God in my awareness. I usually also get out of touch with war torn parts of the world or tragedies in others' lives or how the impoverished and the very ill are living. I remind myself with the following verses what underlies man's 'achievements':

"But the tongue can no man tame; it is an unruly evil, full of

deadly poison." (James 3:8)

"The heart is deceitful above all things, and desperately wicked: who can know it?" (Jeremiah 17:9)

"But without faith, it is impossible to please Him: for he that cometh to God must believe that He is, and that He is a rewarder of them that diligently seek Him." (Hebrews 11:6)

Always the battle cry of the called that leads to **ACTUAL REALITY**:

"And now abideth faith, hope, charity, these three; but the greatest of these is charity." (1 Corinthians 13:13)

Our deliverance from VIRTUAL REALITY:

"Jesus saith unto him, I am the way, the truth, and the life: no man cometh unto the Father, but by Me." (John 14:6)

At times when I want to thank or praise God, and when His grace and its presence I feel:

"This is the day which the Lord hath made; we will rejoice and be glad in it." (Psalm 118:24)

"Now no chastening for the present seemeth to be joyous, but grievous: nevertheless afterward it yieldeth the peaceable fruit of righteousness unto them which are exercised thereby." (Hebrews 12:11)

"Rejoice in the Lord always: and again I say, Rejoice." (Philemon 4:4)

"Let everything that hath breath praise the Lord, Praise ye the Lord." (Psalm 150:6)

"The Lord shall preserve thee from all evil: he shall preserve thy soul. The Lord shall preserve thy going out and thy coming in from this time forth, and even for evermore." (Psalm 121:7-8)

Chapter 14
Flawed But Not Rejected

Of the great men of the Old Testament, I have selected seven to sketch briefly. Adam was the first man and the human father of us all, and set the tone for the human race with all its sin and suffering. Enoch walked with God and never died. Noah was a righteous man who, in effect, became the second human father of us all, but who got carried away with too much of a 'good' thing, which portended things to come. Abraham was the human spiritual father of all Jews, Moslems and Christians, but who had flaws that he had to overcome. Moses delivered God's people to the promised land, but was himself denied entrance. David was a man after God's own heart and whose sin God put away. And Elijah was taken into heaven without seeing death. There are those who, because they are sinful, especially as measured by what the Bible holds up, fear they will never be saved, so why try? They need to think again and have more hope and seek for more faith. Consider this – that almost without exception the men that God chose to be leaders and help accomplish God's will in the world of humanity, were flawed men! We all know about Adam's failure (his disobedience in the Garden of Eden) that doomed the rest of us to sin and death. This led to a terrible condition, *"And God saw that the wickedness of man was great in the earth, and that every imagination of the thoughts of his heart was only evil continually. And it repented the Lord that He had made man on the earth, and it grieved Him at His heart. And the Lord said, I will destroy man whom I have created from the face of the earth; Both man, and beast, and the creeping thing, and the fowls of the air; for it repenteth Me that I have made them. But Noah found grace in the eyes of the Lord."* (Genesis 6:5-8) So Noah built the ark and the floods came and, afterward, Noah's family and the animals emerged from the ark.

When you stop to think of it, Noah was also the father of us all, since the rest of the world perished in the flood. *"And God blessed Noah and his sons, and said unto them, Be fruitful, and multiply, and replenish the earth."* (Genesis 9:1) BUT, after life began returning and his son's families were growing, sin and evil set in once again. Noah, who had a very long life, grew vineyards and developed fermentation of the grape, making wine. He over-imbibed and got drunk and passed out in his tent. His youngest son, Ham, discovered Noah naked in his tent and, instead of respectfully covering him up, he went to his other two brothers and told them what he had seen. This act on Ham's part greatly displeased God and, as a result, God cursed Ham's son, Canaan, and his future generations. And, by the time of the tower of Babel, mankind had gotten so wicked again that God scattered all of the tribes and made them all speak different languages, so they wouldn't have such joint cooperation. This act of God's was because of man's pride, ambition, greed, lust and disobedience, but all that it appeared to do was to slow down man's determination to be a god unto himself or to 'worship' 'gods' who were idols made by human hands who could not talk or move themselves. This same type of credulity is evident in our own times and it takes the form of 'worshipping' human heroes and 'science', such as a 'thoroughgoing' evolutionary worldview. (See pages 159-160.)

I have picked seven of the great men specially appointed by God, in the Old Testament, among hundreds – to show how He picked flawed men in five of the seven cases. The first two were flawed as was the third one, Abraham, who in a different sense of father was the foundation of three religions: Judaism, Islam and Christianity. "Yet this towering figure is frankly portrayed in the Old testament as a flawed, contradictory human being whose personal struggle is a profound and often surprising spiritual drama. Sometimes impatient and deceitful, Abraham comes only slowly to full realization of the true nature of the Lord's revelations and promises to him and to his descendants."[5]

Next is Moses, who brought the Israelites out of Egypt, out of bondage, and to their own promised land, into which Moses was forbidden to enter, after wandering for forty years in the wilderness of Sinaii, because he had not followed God's instructions to the letter. In view of Moses' overall character and obedience, it may seem a harsh sentence, but there may well be more than we know, for God is a just and loving God. Centuries later, Moses appeared to Christ with Elijah, so it was apparent how highly God regarded this great man; but he had human flaws, minor though they were in comparison with the next man of God.

Then, there was David, who reputedly was 'a man after God's own heart', but who sinned grievously (Read 2 Samuel 11:2-17, for the sin of David with Bathsheba), yet because of his undying love for God, *". . . Nathan said unto David, The Lord also hath put away thy sin; thou shalt not die."* (2 Samuel 12:13) David's name appears over a thousand times in the Old and New Testaments, more than anyone else's.[5] To quote from Merrill Unger, "If we proceed to put together, in its most general features, the whole picture of David, which results from all these historical testimonies, we find the very foundations of his character to be laid in peculiarly firm and unshaken trust in Jehovah, and the brightest and most spiritual views of the creation and government of the world, together with a constant, tender, and sensitive awe of the Holy One in Israel, a simple, pure striving never to be untrue to him, and the strongest efforts to return to him all the more loyally after errors and transgressions. . ."[15] So God used and forgave fallible humans, albeit they were exceptional men. Thus, we all have hope of forgiveness and acceptance – but now it must be through the sacrifice of Jesus Christ and the grace of God. *"For by grace are ye saved through faith; and that not of yourselves: it is the gift of God: Not of works, lest any man should boast."* (Ephesians 2:8-9)

The last two men of God are Enoch and Elijah, both of whom talked with God while on this earth and neither of whom ever died. They were both taken up to heaven. Enoch was the seventh from Adam; he lived to be 365 years old and was the father of Methuselah, who was the oldest living man in the Bible, 969 years. We don't know much about Enoch, *"And Enoch walked with God: and he was not for God took him."* (Genesis 5:24) Elijah was one of the greatest prophets and miracle workers of the Old Testament and was used mightily by God over a span of about fifteen years. *"And it came to pass, as they still went on, and talked, that, behold, there appeared a chariot of fire, and horses of fire, and parted them both asunder; and Elijah went up by a whirlwind into heaven."* (2 Kings 2:11) It is said of him, "His faith in God seemed to know no limit nor questioning."[15]

So, there is hope for us, and faith – undeserved but freely given – take it and grow spiritually minded as you reject your carnal mind. There is no greater odyssey in life. Over and over we are shown how flawed is the human race and yet He does not reject us. God's ways are not our ways and we cannot know the mind of God, but we can be sure that mankind was so wicked and evil in the days before the flood that He had no alternative but to destroy all but one family. The Bible says that the day is coming when there will be a final reckoning of mankind. There is a cosmic struggle between good and evil and man, somehow, is in the middle of it without knowing what it is all about. However, you have been informed enough through the Bible and by Jesus Christ and the apostles to make a decision.

"So, as much as in me is, I am ready to preach the gospel to you that are at Rome also. For I am not ashamed of the gospel of Christ: for it is the power of God unto salvation to every one that believeth; to the Jew first, and also to the Greek. For therein is the righteousness of God revealed from faith to faith: as it is written, The just shall live by faith. For the wrath of God is revealed from heaven against all ungodliness and unrighteousness of men, who hold the truth in unrighteousness; Because that which may be known of God is manifest in them; for God hath shewed it unto them. For the invisible things of Him from the creation of the world are clearly seen, being understood by the things that are made, even His eternal power and Godhead; so that they are without excuse: Because that, when they knew God, they glorified Him not as God, neither were thankful; but became vain in their imaginations, and their foolish heart was darkened. Professing themselves to be wise, they became fools, And changed the glory of the uncorruptible God into

an image made like to corruptible man, and to birds, and fourfooted beasts, and creeping things Wherefore God also gave them up to uncleanness through the lusts of their own hearts, to dishonour their own bodies between themselves: Who changed the truth of God into a lie, and worshipped and served the creature more than the Creator, Who is blessed forever. Amen." (Romans 1:15-25)

The two major flaws of the human race, in my belief, are 'human will' and the 'self'. There is no will besides the will of God; any other 'will' is spurious and is of Satan and is counterfeit. Man has freedom to choose between God's Will and delusional will, which is only virtuality – a vapor. There is no Self except God. Even Jesus said, *"I and My Father are one"* (John 10:30) There is only one Existence, one Entity, one BEING, and that is Almighty God, Jesus Christ and the Holy Ghost, Who are one; anything separate is delusional – a vanity. Free will and the self are of Satan and are VIRTUAL REALITY – that is, not reality, but a dream, a delusion, a counterfeit. And it is this VIRTUALITY that we must overcome and reject before we can enter into and become a part of **GOD'S ACTUAL REALITY**. This is impossible without God and requires receiving, accepting and making real the gift of faith from God. Otherwise, our eyes and ears remain closed; therefore, our comprehension and involvement do not become actualized. I believe all the virtuality is inextricably tied in with the dimension of time. Time is a bubble that has 'existence' and 'encapsulates' us but will vanish. We will not, but rather, we will continue on somehow until God's Will is done and we are done with self and become one with God. It is all a matter of faith and practice (being '**receptors**') in this life and this world.

We need Christ and always will. In our present mortal condition in the world of VIRTUAL REALITY, it is my hope that He will forgive us and receive us back no matter whether it be for past, present or future sins, whether they be unknown, known or even knowing sins. Part of my basis for thus believing: 2 Samuel 11:2-17, Luke 15:11-32, Romans 5:6-11, and Romans 7:14-25. (". . . *And Nathan said unto David, The Lord also hath put away thy sin;*

thou shalt not die." 2 Samuel 12:13) (*"For this my son was dead, and is alive again; he was lost, and is found. And they began to be merry."* Luke 15:24) *"For when we were yet without strength, in due time Christ died for the ungodly."* (Romans 5:6) (*"Now if I do that I would not, it is no more I that do it, but sin that dwelleth in me."* Romans 7:20) I, furthermore, believe that this pertains to any and all sins against man. This hope is based on the 'finished work' of Christ, for all believers. (See Matthew 12:31-32 and Luke 12:10.)

Chapter 15
When the End is the Beginning

When we really 'take in' our world and its history, we see that its cosmopolitan cities are actually cesspools of human dereliction, depravity and corruption underlying the glamour and excitement. That science, despite all of its wonders and conveniences, has no warmth for the soul. We are winners if we trade enjoyment of 'life' (i.e., carnal life) for the joy and inner warmth of the love of God.

There is an ubiquitous force trying constantly to distract one; consider not only television, sports and other forms of 'entertainment', but also how the mind wanders when reading or listening to the Bible as opposed to the rapt attention one gives to gossip and bad news.

It is absolutely vital that we allow to sink in, how horrible and pervasive sin and evil are, during our sojourn on earth. Further, how far our rational mind falls short in overcoming the willful, rebellious 'selfness'. We must wait upon God; we need to love, honor and exalt Him in our lives, because only He can change us and then only if we invite Him to do this.

Christianity is a full-time lifestyle and, in a way, an all or nothing faith. *"I know thy works, that thou art neither cold nor hot: I would thou wert cold or hot. So then because thou art lukewarm, and neither cold nor hot, I will spue thee out of My mouth."* (Revelation 3:15-16) Even though no one can pursue it or live it perfectly or even consistently, it is this very aspect that confirms the need of Christ's life, death and resurrection to satisfy God's justice and His ability to accept us, flawed though we are. It is because of the GRACE of God that He offers His love to us and enables us to grow in faith if so we desire. We are not deserving of it and it is important that we see the need for our redemption through Jesus Christ and sanctification through the Holy Spirit of God. God's strength is made perfect in our weakness even as it was with the great men of the Bible. As pointed out in the previous chapter, the

Bible does not varnish or whitewash its heroes; it tells it like it is, like we humans are. We need to keep foremost in our mind, as we fight the battle of faith in this enticing world, that we will have failures and setbacks in our life of faith – but when we do, we have to recover and renew our faith in God and His mercy and love. Above all, we must not reject who we are or give up. Each of us is a unique individual to whom God offers love and immortality.

In Christianity, 'losing' is winning. That is, denying (losing) yourself, taking up your cross (rejecting the world) and following Christ, is the way to immortal life with God. *"For all that is in the world, the lust of the flesh, and the lust of the eyes, and the pride of life, is not of the Father, but is of the world."* (1 John 2:16) It seems clear to me that Jesus Christ is the **ACTUAL REALITY** of God in our VIRTUAL REALITY, *"I and My Father are one."* (John 10:30) Further, *"And he that seeth Me seeth Him that sent Me."* (John 12:45) Jesus refers to Himself with the identical phrase that God referred to Himself in the Old Testament: *"Jesus said unto them, Verily, verily, I say unto you, Before Abraham was, I am."* (John 8:58) *"And God said unto Moses, I am that I am: and He said, Thus shalt thou say unto the children of Israel, I am hath sent me unto you."* (Exodus 3:14) Now that Jesus is no longer here on earth, God has sent the Holy Ghost or His Holy Spirit (also called the Comforter) to us. *"But the Comforter, which is the Holy Ghost, whom the Father will send in My name, He shall teach you all things, and bring all things to your remembrance, whatsoever I have said unto you."* (John 14:26)

"Jesus saith unto him, I am the way, the truth, and the life: no man cometh unto the Father, but by Me." (John 14:6) What does that mean? St. Paul instructs us in his letters to the Romans and to the Galatians, as follows, *"And not only so, but we glory in tribulations also: knowing that tribulation worketh patience; and patience, experience; and experience, hope: And hope maketh not ashamed; because the love of God is shed abroad in our hearts by the Holy Ghost which is given unto us."* (Romans 5:3-5) *"But the fruit of the Spirit is love, joy, peace, longsuffering, gentleness, good-*

ness, faith, Meekness, temperance: against such there is no law." (Galatians 5:22-23) St. Peter tells us, *"And beside this, giving all diligence, add to your faith virtue; and to virtue knowledge; and to knowledge temperance; and to temperance patience; and to patience godliness; And to godliness brotherly kindness; and to brotherly kindness charity. For if these things be in you, and abound, they make you that ye shall neither be barren nor unfruitful in the knowledge of our Lord Jesus Christ. But he that lacketh these things is blind, and cannot see afar off, and hath forgotten that he was purged from his old sins. Wherefore the rather, brethren, give diligence to make your calling and election sure: for if ye do these things, ye shall never fall: For so an entrance shall be ministered unto you abundantly into the everlasting kingdom of our Lord and Saviour Jesus Christ."* (2 Peter 1:5-11)

And it is under these circumstances that the end (of earthly carnal living), becomes the beginning (of immortal spiritual life). Jesus has already defeated Satan and sin. We can, therefore, accept His victory and allow it to make Satan's ongoing attempts to manipulate and defeat us, ineffectual. Just allow God's peace and joy to fill us – replacing the consternation and futility of involvement with Satan who is already defeated. Thus, we can let Jesus' finished work free our minds from Satan's deceitful efforts and we can live in Christ's accomplished work. No more need sin frustrate and defeat us, as Satan's VIRTUAL REALITY is an illusion. Know this and live in the peace and joy of God's **ACTUAL REALITY**.

Let not sin continue to control us – we can ignore and reject our 'old man' (our carnal mind) with its bad deeds and evil thoughts. In Christ, we are already free; let the Comforter guide us. This is not a victory that we have to win (or even can win); the Lord has already done it. We must let go of pride and vain effort – it is not only an impossible effort, but unnecessary. A believer is still partly controlled by the illusion of sin, a saint (in this book's definition of saint) has dispelled the mirage of sin, and a non-believer is still fast in the grip of Satan and the delusion of sin. We must wake up and put off the 'old man' before it is too late. Following are pertinent quotations referring to this: *"Knowing this, that our old man is crucified with Him, that the body of sin might be destroyed, that henceforth we should not serve sin."* (Romans 6:6) *"But ye have not so learned Christ; If so be that ye have heard Him, and have been taught by Him, as the truth is in Jesus: That ye put off concerning the former conversation the old man, which is corrupt according to the deceitful lusts; And be renewed in the spirit of your mind; And that ye put on the new man, which after God is created in righteousness and true holiness."* (Ephesians 4:20-24) *"Lie not one to another, seeing that ye have put off the old man with his deeds; And have put on the new man, which is renewed in knowledge after the image of Him that created him: Where there is neither Greek nor Jew, circumcision nor uncircumcision, Barbarian, Scythian, bond nor free: but Christ is all, and in all."* (Colossians 3:9-11)

If you believe and practice the foregoing, then the end of your mortal, earthly life will truly be the beginning of your immortal, spiritual life. You may wonder, why you are not aware of God's response, or do not seem to be 'in touch' with the Holy Spirit. Set aside that doubt or fear; hope is an essential part of faith. *"For we know that the whole creation groaneth and travaileth in pain together until now. And not only they, but ourselves also, which have the first fruits of the Spirit, even we ourselves groan within ourselves, waiting for the adoption, to wit, the redemption of our body. For we are saved by hope: but hope that is seen is not hope: for what a man seeth, why doth he yet hope for? But if we hope for that we see not, then do we with patience wait for it."* (Romans 8:22-25) Hope is such an essential part of faith and faith is indispensable to being chosen by God for salvation and immortality.

"NOW faith is the substance of things hoped for, the evidence of things not seen." (Hebrews 11:1) So, we need to hold on to our hope and our faith no matter what. When we do, we begin to acknowledge God in the little things. He is always helping us and we must believe that, even to the point of finding a 'parking space', we need to see His presence in all aspects of our life. *"That they*

should seek the Lord, if haply they might feel after Him, and find Him, though He be not far from every one of us: For in Him we live, and move, and have our being; as certain also of your own poets have said, For we are also His offspring." (Acts 17:27-28) As we do this, we begin to feel His presence more and more, and it is evident in such things as a sense of peace, sometimes a feeling of joy, and we may feel a physical sense of relaxation in our bodies – at times almost a euphoric feeling. But we must believe He is and that He is with us, in us and for us. Then a sense of 'knowing' makes itself felt more often and our hearts are really softened and, gradually, we are enabled (by the Holy Spirit) to live the virtues Christ outlined for us. Please read again the 'progression' of our spiritual growth as described earlier in this chapter. For example, where St. Paul pointed out, among other things, "*. . . that tribulation worketh patience; and patience, experience; and experience, hope: And hope maketh not ashamed; because the love of God is shed abroad in our hearts by the Holy Ghost which is given unto us."* (Romans 5:3-5) Peter also tells us in 2 Peter 1:5-11, quoted earlier in this chapter, some of the virtues that we build on in this Christian growth. But there is no growth without faith and hope – which do lead to our becoming more loving, even to people who mistreat us.

Please bear in mind, also, that when we pray for something and don't get it (or think our prayer isn't answered), especially if some 'misfortune' befalls us or even the reverse of what we have prayed for occurs; if we are trying to be in touch with God and endeavoring to make our faith stronger, then hold in your mind, *"And we know that all things work together for good to them that love God, to them who are the called according to His purpose."* (Romans 8:28) 'Know' that you are 'the called' and 'see' God's presence everywhere, read the Bible, pray, thanking and praising Him (prayer is not just for making some request).

If you feel unworthy or too 'bad' to be 'called', look at the men God has dealt with all through the Bible (some were pointed out in Chapter 14). When Jesus called Peter to follow Him, this is the response according to Gardner and Associates[5], "Peter's immediate response was one of unworthiness and fear: *'He fell down at Jesus' knees, saying, Depart from me, for I am a sinful man, O Lord'* (Luke 5:8), But Jesus would not depart. It was precisely such a person, a man who knew his own weakness and sinfulness but could recognize and acknowledge the presence of God's power, that Jesus wanted." To quote later on in the same section, "The Gospels often present Peter as a paradigm of both vigorous faith and human uncertainty and doubts." Peter denied Christ three times just before His trial and yet Christ associated him with the founding of His church, calling Peter the 'rock' upon which His church would be built (Peter means rock in Greek). So take heart, and do not allow Satan (your adversary) to break down your faith and hope when you have fallen back into some sinful thoughts or act. Redouble your efforts and renew your faith and your hope. *"Be sober, be vigilant; because your adversary the devil, as a roaring lion, walketh about, seeking whom he may devour: Whom resist steadfast in the faith, knowing that the same afflictions are accomplished in your brethren that are in the world."* (1 Peter 5:8-9)

All of our known world are creations of God, part of which are also representations of God, such as mankind, angels, etc. Humans, on the other hand, produce things by inspiration from God; they also produce representations of themselves, that is, children. And, no matter how 'good' you are (industrious, rational, healthy, moral, and understanding), you have only a limited control over your children regarding what they will become as adults (accomplishments, behavior, personality, health).This is because your treatment of them (discipline, training, love and the example of your behavior after which they model themselves to some degree), only partly influences them. There are other forces at work 'shaping' them, such as peers, teachers, illness and other life experiences. In addition, you have little control over their genes, which have vital impacts in many areas. Furthermore, there are characteristics, behavior, talents and flaws that we and science cannot account for. It may be that transcending influence of Free Choice, or each of us may be a by-product of (i.e., incidental) or the results of (directly involved) cosmic forces and/or cosmic conflict.

Nevertheless, you as a parent may exercise more direct control over the molding of your child than God does. He has not only given us, but also our children, Free Choice. Your child does not understand why you discipline him at times, or why you treat him the way you do at other times (I am here speaking of concerned, intelligent and loving treatment and discipline).* Taking this to an exponentially higher level, how can we possibly understand what happens to us, or in the world? Yet we are apt to judge God as being 'irresponsibly' responsible! This can throw a new light on why faith is so basic to Christianity. (*"But without faith it is impossible to please Him: . . ."* [Hebrews 11:6]) We must believe what Christ said about God and about how we should live. Our faith is shown by our obedience, i.e., our 'walk'. To grasp the Old Testament is even further beyond our ken. But within the New Testament, we can agree with and understand that Christ's 'way' would lead to a better world, yet we still resist. The imperative remains: you must have faith in God, and hope is a necessary (but not sufficient) ingredient.

The word faith means complete assurance and certitude regarding the character, ability, strength, or truth of someone or something. Christian faith means believing in Christ and his definition of and pronouncements about God, for example, that He is love and He deals with us individually and personally. Christian faith is the only means of salvation for those that have heard Christ's message, read the New Testament or have heard the Word preached or discussed. AND, it has to be a working, living faith, imperfect though it is. Now is the time to start working in the sense of accepting Jesus Christ, putting the love of God first in your life and the love of your fellow man second ('you' meaning you and your spouse as 'one'), so that your earthly 'end' will be the real beginning of immortality as God planned it for you.

*If you have children, or plan to, you need to, as Christians, lovingly accept sacrifice and denial of many of your interests and needs for the first eighteen years of your children's lives. Mother or father should remain in the home and both should spend more time and interest with the family and less at work, while at the same time maintaining a compatible relationship with each other. If this seems impossible, live prayerfully.

Chapter 16
Where Is Hell?

Many people wonder about hell. Is there such a 'place'; is it a state of being; where is it if it does exist? Sometimes it seems as if 'this life is hell', or 'we are already living in hell'. The common Christian conception is that if there is a hell, it is in our future if we are unrepentant sinners. Generally, there is much controversy or, at least, different opinions as to what it takes to consign a person to hell, what it is, where it is, what it is like, how long it lasts, or does it even exist? *"I Am He that liveth, and was dead; and, behold, I Am alive for evermore, Amen; and have the keys of hell and of death."* (Revelation 1:18) *"He that hath an ear, let him hear what the Spirit saith unto the churches; To him that overcometh will I give to eat of the tree of life, which is in the midst of the paradise of God."* (Revelation 2:7)

"He that hath an ear, let him hear what the Spirit saith unto the churches; He that overcometh shall not be hurt of the second death." (Revelation 2:11) *"And the devil that deceived them was cast into the lake of fire and brimstone, where the beast and the false prophet are, and shall be tormented day and night for ever and ever."* (Revelation 20:10) *"And the sea gave up the dead which were in it; and death and hell delivered up the dead which were in them: and they were judged every man according to their works. And death and hell were cast into the lake of fire. This is the second death. And whosoever was not found written in the book of life was cast into the lake of fire."* (Revelation 20:13-15)

"And He said unto me, It is done. I Am Alpha and Omega, the beginning and the end. I will give unto him that is athirst of the fountain of the water of life freely. He that overcometh shall inherit all things; and I will be his God, and he shall be My son. But the fearful, and unbelieving, and the abominable and murderers, and whoremongers, and sorcerers, and idolaters, and all liars, shall have their part in the lake which burneth with fire and brimstone: which is the second death." (Revelation 21:6-8)

Thus, there is an actual place called hell, although it may be in the spiritual realm. Hell is a place that will ultimately be destroyed by being cast into the 'lake of fire', which obviously, therefore, is not itself hell. It is my interpretation that hell also exists for any person anywhere, anytime that he is without God. I believe that a person can be in hell while still alive on this earth – as well as after death. Those that think they are in hell, here and now, may be. If they do not have faith in God, they are in hell no matter what the outward appearances. The Lord said, *"Neither shall they say, Lo here! or, lo there! for, behold, the kingdom of God is within you."* (Luke 17:21)

On the contrary, those who, to all outward appearances, are rich and famous, powerful and successful, may already be in hell (if they have not Christ in their hearts), even though they may deny this to themselves. However, other people (spouses, house servants, close business associates, personal physicians and psychotherapists) can see the frenetic pace, paranoias, phobias, anxieties and doubts that already beset them. *"And Jesus looked round about, and saith unto His disciples, How hardly shall they that have riches enter into the kingdom of God!"* (Mark 10:23)

The multitudes, are the undecided, the 'lukewarms', and the uncommitted. These people either deny reality, and are living in VIRTUAL REALITY, or they have deceived themselves into believing that they are committed. They have never approached beginning to know that an **ACTUAL REALITY** does exist and so cannot contrast their VIRTUAL REALITY with any grasp or comprehension of **ACTUAL REALITY**. These are the ones who don't know that they don't know because it takes a leap of faith to begin to get in touch with **ACTUAL REALITY**.

It seems to me that Adam went immediately from paradise into hell the minute he disobeyed God and partook of the forbidden fruit, for he lost touch with God. *"And they heard the voice of the Lord God walking in the garden in the cool of the day: and Adam and his wife hid themselves from the presence of the Lord God amongst the trees of the garden. And the Lord God called unto Adam, and said unto him, Where art thou?"* (Genesis 3:8-9) 'All hell broke loose', so to speak; Adam's oldest son killed his younger brother, and things kept going downhill thereafter, culminating in the flood, whereby God destroyed all humans, except Noah's family, because of the sinfulness of the human race. That is what happens when man gets separated from God.

The only two humans that never saw death, but instead were taken up by God (Enoch and Elijah), both walked and talked with God! So they were already in paradise while on this earth, they were so close to God. *"And Enoch walked with God: and he was not; for God took him."* (Genesis 5:24) *"And it came to pass, as they still went on, and talked, that, behold, there appeared a chariot of fire, and horses of fire, and parted them both asunder; and Elijah went up by a whirlwind into heaven."* (2 Kings 2:11)

Life is hell – without God! What does it take for that message to get through? How much does a person have to suffer before the truth begins to dawn? An actual hell may have to exist for some before they really reach for God through faith in Jesus Christ. Christians may suffer for a different reason. *"Fear none of those things which thou shalt suffer: behold, the devil shall cast some of you into prison, that ye may be tried; and ye shall have tribulation ten days: be thou faithful unto death, and I will give thee a crown of life. He that hath an ear, let him hear what the Spirit saith unto the churches; He that overcometh shall not be hurt of the second death."* (Revelation 2:10-11)

But listen to these words of Christ: *"These things I have spoken unto you, that in Me ye might have peace. In the world ye shall have tribulation: but be of good cheer; I have overcome the world."* (John 16:33) How much better to bear our cross here and now in this life and this world with Christ in our heart. In other words, we will have our cross to bear, but if, at the same time, we have the kingdom of heaven in our heart, the cross will be 'light'. 'Heaven' can begin here and now – God is waiting. Just as the sun sheds his light, so God will shed His love in our hearts – day and night! He is just waiting for us to ask for His presence and guidance, then to seek Him and finally to allow Him to enter in when He opens our heart to His love. We are then entering the end of our life in VIRTUAL REALITY and beginning to enter His **ACTUAL REALITY**.

At our stage on earth, our reliance is on faith for reassurance, as we do not see Him nor talk with Him. Yet we 'know' and are increasingly blessed with other spiritual fruit, such as love, joy, patience, gentleness, kindness, etc.

Why is love so important and necessary ? As I see it, love is the only thing that can overcome evil and even destroy evil if necessary, because love is the perfect passion, and so it must also contain justice. Whereas Jesus Christ took our judgment upon Himself, Satan will be destroyed by the justice of perfect love – since he rejects love and is unrepentant.

Empathy is another part of love and, without empathy, we could not love each other because we humans are such a mess: sinning, grasping, lusting, self-serving, resentful, angry, hateful and violent. As we make mistakes and hurt loved ones thoughtlessly, we begin to understand the actions of others who go through the same experiences or commit the same deviant behavior as we do. Once we can thus identify with a transgressor, we are able to 'feel' for him and 'forgive' him, and even to love him. Without empathy, that would be impossible and, I believe (since Adam's 'fall' and man's separation from God), we are only able to empathize with another because we first make mistakes. Thus, being a race of sinners, we must be able to generalize our experiences to others in order to feel compassion for them. Therefore, love is absolutely vital in this world inhabited by sinners, otherwise we would murder each other off, being filled only with disdain or hate for everyone else. However, we cannot generalize love to enough others to make any significant difference without the Holy Spirit. God's love overcomes and wins against evil. We are dealing with Satan whom Christ has defeated, but who is still active in this era or dispensation. It is my understanding of the Bible that God, our Creator; Jesus Christ, our Saviour; and the Holy Ghost, our Sanctifier; are all manifestations of Almighty God.

Not until we see how lost we are and mired in sin can we be loving toward our enemies. Then, we can begin to see the need to be loving toward everyone as well as our own need for redemption. There is (from my reading of the bible) an actual hell where suffering is unmitigated for a time and from which people can be retrieved. There is also a hell on earth, which resides in the mind and the heart, independent of external circumstances. Hell is in VIRTUAL REALITY; **ACTUAL REALITY** is in God.

What we have to realize is that, as humans, we are so vulnerable and we are not captains of our own destinies on the world stage, but rather are susceptible to all the vagaries that biological life is heir to, as well as the dangers of this modern world of man (read that, Satan). As perishable a commodity as modern man is, he can still puff up his ego enough to feel invincible. Too often, it is not until some tragedy strikes that some humans think more seriously of the meaning and purpose of our life in the here and now and place credence in God and the Bible. In the 'Inaugural Issue' of *George* (October/November 1995) the Editor-in-Chief, John F. Kennedy, Jr., interviewed George Wallace, former Governor of Alabama, and asked Mr. Wallace, who was severely wounded (confined to a wheelchair and in severe pain) by the bullets of a would-be assassin's gun, the following question. "JK: When did you become born-again? GW: When I was shot. It was then that I saw how fragile life was and how short it might be, so I realized you'd better be prepared to die at any time."

Where God is, there is love. Where God is not, there is hell. If you suffer reversals, misfortune, hardship, accidents, illness or any kind of affliction and tribulation; if you are a Christian, you are not in hell, nor are you being punished. As St. Paul states, *"For which cause we faint not; but though our outward man perish, yet the inward man is renewed day by day. For our light affliction, which is but for a moment, worketh for us a far more exceeding and eternal weight of glory; While we look not at the things which are seen, but at the things which are not seen: for the things which are seen are temporal; but the things which are not seen are eternal."* (2 Corinthians 4:16-18) And St. John quotes Jesus, *"These things I have spoken unto you, that in Me ye might have peace. In the world ye shall have tribulation: but be of good cheer; I have overcome the world."* (John 16: 33)

Chapter 17
Secret of Life

"For the law of the Spirit of life in Christ Jesus hath made me free from the law of sin and death." (Romans 8:2)

It is not self-confidence that is needed or that is lacking, in fact **it** is the problem. Blaming a lack of self-confidence for failure really obscures the underlying and basic difficulty, which is a lack of 'God-confidence' or faith, in other words. The fault lies precisely with inserting the self between God and you. The least this does is to obscure what God wants for your life and in what direction you should go. You are God's creation and this is God's universe; if you are lost, it is because you have either turned away from God or you were never really in a relationship with Him.

The vital thing for your life and your loved ones is to get in touch with Him, and this can only be done by believing in Him and having faith (which is a gift from Him, if you will look for it, want it and accept it), and living in faith. This means always turning to Him, seeking His will and His guidance – inwardly. This is a growth process and entails increasingly trying and trusting in His presence and His constant flow of blessings to you. This you must assume, accept and act upon. It is ironic that when you are involved with 'self' you end up damning your 'self', which inappropriately but inevitably has become confused with your identity, your individuality, i.e., who you are; and this is a terrible travesty of reality – a perversion.

When you 1) fail to feel His presence or 2) deliberately not seek Him or 3) doubt His acceptance of you because it seems so intangible or unlikely, it is absolutely necessary to push aside the doubt AND the self-damning. Get self out of the picture! Self is at the base of all difficulties in this life and is what separates you

[Note: The use of the pronoun *you* is used in the generic sense, as it is more powerful and more general than it would be to bounce between I, me, we, us, you; especially when talking about the entity *self*.]

from God. By the very nature of faith, a nearly continuous struggle with doubt is present in the beginning and, therefore, hope is the only thing it seems that you have to hold on to at times. But hold on to it; without hope, the battle is lost. And you will probably lose many battles, but only through doubt, disbelief and self will you lose the war. The less you are self-centered, the more you become God-centered, and the more you are enabled to become loving, the way He wants you to be. HOWEVER, this entire process hinges on your having faith in God, because of and through Jesus Christ. That is why He is called a 'stumbling block' to the Jews and 'foolishness' to the Greeks (and here 'Greeks' signify all non-Jews). But in Christ, there is neither Jew nor Greek, as all believers are one. Christian faith is belief, to the degree of conviction – to the extent of 'knowing', to the certainty of staking your life, your peace, your joy and your energy on God, His word, His promises and His Son, Jesus Christ. So faith is not a matter of faith in yourself or in self-confidence, but rather in God-confidence, i.e., faith in God that He is what He claims and does what He promises.

Even after we have 'accepted' Christ – or believe in Him and feel or think we have been 'born again', we still keep failing and falling back into error. We will always need God's forgiveness and acceptance through Jesus – that is why He came and why, after He left, He sent the Holy Ghost. We are not perfect and, I believe, will not be in this life. We must strive to please God by obedience, by denying our self and following Christ. But we cannot do it on our own, and we must die to self and take up our cross before we will ever be perfect, as God is perfect, (one with God). I do not believe it will be in this carnal world or with a carnal mind and body.

Because of Jesus, if you have faith in Him, you will become more and more loving, because it is God Who sheds His love in your heart – enabling you to love Him back as well as loving others, even your enemies. Jesus Christ is your only hope and you must hang on to hope; He will never let you go. He will always be there for you. BUT, you must know that and remind yourself that it is not dependent upon you – He did it all for you – just have faith in

Him and He that sent Him, and the doubt and despair that Satan tries to constantly infect you with, diminishes and disappears.

The devil does not give up trying to defeat your faith. But he cannot succeed, as long as you trust Jesus, seek the Holy Ghost and let God's love spread forth from you. This is a testing time in the sense of learning to lose your self and to find God. When your faith is low, increase your hope and your faith will re-emerge. More and more, the fruit of the Spirit will be present with you: love, joy, peace, patience, gentleness, goodness, faith, temperance and humility. These money cannot buy and power cannot bring about.

We all experience the vagaries of life; take them as they come in perfect reliance on and confidence in God that He will take care of all. We are to be unmoved and unshaken in our faith that all is with His knowledge and nothing, nothing can separate us from Him, and that someday, no matter what we experience, we will be with Him. All that we accomplish is from Him; all that we fail is of no matter as long as we wait on and trust in Him.

We must rely upon Christ's crucifixion and resurrection for our salvation. By the time we arrive at a living faith in God, in Jesus Christ and in the Holy Spirit, we often have become embroiled in an unchristian lifestyle or, in one way or another, we cannot cleanse ourselves from all sinning, to the 'letter of the spirit'. At this juncture, we must call upon our faith in the nature of God, that He is indeed loving and therefore able, through Christ, to 'put away' not only our sins but our sinning. It would be nice if things were black and white; but they are not. A simplistic approach to life is convenient but unrealistic, and some fundamentalists get caught in that trap and end up by judging others and becoming 'exclusive', in the sense of 'us against them'. We may not be able to become as 'purely spiritual a being' as we want or that we know Christ would want us to be, sometimes just because other people (loved ones) have become involved and we cannot make the changes we 'know' we should without hurting them. Perhaps this is a demonstration of our lack of really trusting God's love and His ability. Perhaps, in the end, it is just an excuse, and we may be involved in self-deception. At any rate, the bottom line is, we are not perfect and we need to put aside self and rely on Jesus Christ's sacrifice and God's love.

To illustrate the above, suppose you are a prostitute and, although you hate the 'work' and you detest being a whore, you continue because you know of no other way to give your children a chance in life. Or, perhaps you are a drug dealer, and the best you can do is to limit the drugs to marijuana; you refuse to deal in cocaine or heroin, but it lies heavy on your heart that you (although you have a legitimate daytime job) are breaking the law. However, you know (or think you know), that if you gave up that income, there would be no chance for your children to go to the proper schools or associate with peers that had all the advantages and who would be a future network for your children to call upon for favors. Or maybe you are a 'yes' man fearful of losing your job in a company with disreputable practices. Certainly this is a lack of faith, but the point I am trying to make is that we humans are all such a 'mess' and so deluded that, without God's ongoing forgiveness and guidance, we are lost.

An example that could apply to a lot of people today would be a person who has become a 'born-again' Christian, and he or she has had one or two divorces and is married to a non-believing person with whom children have been conceived; He or she cannot undo the past and cannot correct the present or future without hurting loved ones – in this case who is to say that it is unchristian to stay with the present spouse or that it would be selfish and self-centered to leave the spouse? Is there an answer? Yes: faith in God's love, guidance and forgiveness through Jesus Christ.

It is in the sense of the above passages that one must look at the world situation. If anything is a mess, it is the way humans treat other humans. It doesn't really matter if it is a capitalistic or a communistic system (or any human system). Underlying man's inhumanity to man are greed, power, control and hedonism; in other words, *self*. The only salvation for the world lies in love, peace, goodness, gentleness, patience, temperance, humility, joy and faith.

BUT, these things are impossible on a working scale without God. Which means we can only accomplish this through God and in God's way.

It is possible to agree, among most people – and it doesn't matter whether a person is liberal, conservative, democrat or republican, white or black or brown or red or yellow, American or foreigner – that the good qualities outlined above are essential. The problems of the world lie in the bad qualities outlined in the same paragraph. Even so, humans have never been able to develop a world, or even a society, that embodies this common 'wisdom'. And they never will!!!

It is obvious from history that even though this knowledge was known from ancient Greece – in fact from the eating of the apple in the Garden of Eden – man is not capable of bringing about an earthly paradise. It is only by following the teachings of Christ and acceptance of Him that this will eventually be experienced by 'believers' and 'saints'. For one thing, knowledge of good and evil is not enough! I believe that only through God's intervention on a universal scale, with the death of carnal knowledge and the end of physical living, will the immortality of spiritual life occur. That is, the replacement of VIRTUAL REALITY with **ACTUAL REALITY**!

When have you taken the time to dwell on the presence of God or think about the meaning of life? As minimally as turning off the car radio or skipping a television program?

I truly believe that the sooner one turns to Jesus in faith, the more noble and the more fulfilling life will be, in the here and now, not only in the hereafter. I surmise that a 'saint' will have some significance that a 'believer' will not in our coming spiritual lives. Be that as it may, there is no question in my mind that everyone who turns to Christ and struggles with faith, reaching that point where God's love is a real presence, begins to live in **ACTUAL REALITY**, in the here and now, and that is a foretaste of glory.

Love, gifted from God through Christian faith, kept alive by hope, enabled by the Holy Spirit, is the secret of life immortal.

Chapter 18
Mortal Combat

Much of the basis upon which the American Democracy was built derived from the Biblical admonitions that the head of man was God, and the head of the family was man. Both of these tenets were either held or practiced by our founding fathers, but are being more and more eroded. The consequences surround us in today's American culture and society, threatening to engulf us in a deepening morass of immorality, anarchy and crime. It is time to get back to the Bible and back to mothering and fathering. It is either the reestablishment of authority and love in the home, or it is the decline, decay, devastation and depression that will take over our future. However, this must be an individual effort and not forced upon any adult. It needs to be a **non-violent web** of individuals as described on page 94. The New Testament is a manifesto for a personal civil war, a war between two opposing and incompatible states of mind, one carnal – which is self-seeking and fatally parasitizing to its possessor, the other spiritual – which is self-denying and gloriously immortalizes its possessor, in the event of its triumph. This is, however, a war to the end. There is no truce or compromise. I believe only in this life can the two even inhabit the same person and, unfortunately, it is a tacit enmity which the individual can easily ignore or deny, in which case the ending is in an ignominious mortality.

This life on earth is a journey, the purpose of which is for aliens (you and me) to complete our odyssey successfully by becoming spiritually minded. This occurs through allowing himself or herself to be molded into the man or woman that God originally created, in essence, perfect, but which could somehow only become a reality through the struggle of existing with free choice in a mind that was already carnal. Through the grace of God, you can utilize this opportunity to become self-less and to overcome evil with love, i.e., 'becoming' totally spiritually minded and, thereby fulfilling the 'essence' which is the man and woman that God created, in our beginning. Thereafter, he or she becomes a 'new man' or 'new woman' and is born a citizen into a 'new world'. This represents a mystery in that, somehow, this period of carnality (on earth) was necessary as a step in the 'forming' of humans that would never again be vulnerable to evil. Perhaps this struggle between carnality and spirituality was necessary to learn, while possessing free choice, that exalting self and attempting to become independent of God is death and hell. Once through this metamorphosis, I believe, the Spiritual being called man or woman can exist in any and all forms or states (physical, spiritual and probably other states of being we know nothing about), unbounded by time or space. It would seem that to be 'perfect', i.e., the essence that God created, in any existence or function, we must be free to choose, and in order to have a choice, there must be evil and, further, we must know right from wrong, and both want to choose right and be enabled to do so.

The purpose of human life is to change from carnal to spiritual creatures as defined by and through Jesus Christ, Who has conquered carnality, sin and death. God, our Creator, will enable us to do this through faith in Him. This does not mean we will not suffer, but He will be with us and, even if we die, we will live again spiritually, immortally and with joy – i.e., **ACTUAL REALITY**. The New Testament is our handbook on how to survive and conquer this carnal world. The Holy Spirit of God is given to us and remains with us always, even though we may not understand, at times, what is happening. That is where faith plays an essential part. He gives us hope, as He gives us faith, by His grace – His gifts are free and unearned as well as undeserved. Thus, He demonstrates love to us and through us – however, and this is a mystery, He has chosen us before we are born, yet we must respond before we die.

There may be evil humans and there is an evil counter force, Satan, involved in a cosmic battle for the heart and soul; mind and spirit of humans. Each person has a choice of whose side to be on and whether or not to opt for this carnal life of VIRTUAL REAL-

ITY or whether to commit to faith in Jesus Christ for a better life, a better way, and the ultimate truth, **ACTUAL REALITY**. We cannot judge others for no one knows what another mind is becoming – holy and spiritual or carnal and ultimately evil. We cannot judge on what we see or what we hear. We are to love all people. We are engaged in the ultimate challenge of overcoming evil with selfless love. Only with God's Spirit can we win and, by this route alone, will we come to our new homeland and **be**.

Presently, we are in the process of 'becoming' what God intended us to become; if not, then we are failing and perishing – no matter how handsome, wealthy, healthy, happy, powerful or adored we are on earth. It is fatal to mistakenly equate a materialistic life of ease and plenty as a sign that God is blessing us, especially if it is not accompanied with His spiritual gifts. On the other hand, it is an insidious and ubiquitous technique of Satan to make us doubt God and His approval of us on the basis of our being in a state of poverty, poor health, or oppression. God is always there for us. We need to see through the Satanic deceit of the VIRTUAL REALITY of this present world and begin to enter God's **ACTUAL REALITY**, which He created for us from the beginning.

However, it appears more and more that there is 'one world' coming that will be ruled by international corporations (banking, manufacturing, retailing, entertainment, communications and service). If this happens, it will be the epitome of a carnal world and the people will be ruled by these conglomerates and cartels – a world of VIRTUAL REALITY. The United States has always been a God-fearing nation, at least in its public proclamations as well as having a large part of its middle class professing Christian beliefs and values. I refer again to Stanton Evan's book, *The Theme is Freedom*[3]. It would seem that God has truly blessed America. I say 'seem' because it is not clear to me how much God blesses in carnal ways. (See Romans 8:7.) However, the Bible states that all power comes from God (see Romans Chapter 13). The least one could say would be that, by and large, God has blessed us with good leaders. Despite our 'glorious' living standards or in part, because of them, we as a nation are teetering on the brink of abandoning God. It would be a good practice to look at our leaders and do everything in our individual power (vote and participate in school boards, etc.), to assure that we have God-fearing leaders.* Inventions and improvements in manufacturing, entertainment, conveniences, communications, transportation and medicine, are fine, but they all deal with the physical body. The body is destined to die. Only the spirit lives on, so why not begin to focus on the spirit and grow Spiritually. Once you start to do that, it doesn't matter what becomes of your body, as you become more Spiritually minded, you begin to possess immortality and to surmount time and matter; you are at the entrance of **ACTUAL REALITY**.

The latest bit of 'wizardry' from the marvels of science is the simulated reality created by the software, hardware and peripherals of computers combined with other things, such as television and communication systems. But, it is still not the real thing; it is as if we are actually 'advancing' further and further away from **ACTUAL REALITY** and making it harder and harder to believe in God. *Newsweek* of 2/27/95 features 'Technomania' in an article on page 29 by Steven Levy follows, by way of illustration. "As Nicholas Negroponti, of M.I.T.'s media Lab, puts it, the essence of the information revolution is the difference between atoms and bits. The former are the building blocks for physical stuff, which until now has formed the basis of our economy as well as our consciousness. Bits, however, are ephemeral – they are simply ones and zeros. From that slight scaffolding, we have the bounty of the information age: all the documents, spreadsheets, audio CDs, multimedia CD-ROMs, movie special effects and virtual-reality environments. As more of our experience comes to us by way of bits, reality itself gradually changes. Literally out of nothing, a new dimension emerges: cyberspace, a place made out of bits, whose intangible nature does not prevent it from becoming a second home, or a primary workplace, for masses of infonauts." (See Chapter 19 for more on cyberspace.)

Thus, strangely enough, we physical beings are developing a

world for ourselves that is becoming more and more ethereal, with 'bits' and the growing VIRTUAL REALITY of our computerized society. However, that is not to be mistaken for Spirituality, ephemeral as it may be. Once again, man is trying (perhaps unknowingly, as in pawns of the devil) to duplicate what God created but, as always, it is counterfeit. We have the seed of spirituality in us, but are dominated by our 'natural' nature (or our carnality), and the warfare goes on between good and evil – spiritual and physical (carnal). It is a mortal combat, and most humans are unaware of or deny God's reality, i.e., **ACTUAL REALITY**.

*It is said that a nation gets the leaders it deserves (i.e., the 'times' create the leader rather than the leader creating the 'times'). This is a chilling thought. Think about it!

Chapter 19
Enemy Within

The following quote is from the October 5, 1995 issue of *The New York Times* article titled 'Cyberspace Trips to Nowhere Land', by Paul Goldberger (pages B-1 and B-4): "We hear continually about cyberspace as a place of connections made between all kinds of people who would not have come together before. Perhaps. But every one of them has connected by being alone, in front of a computer screen, and this is a poor excuse for what community has meant for most of history. . .But then, this is no real village, no real city, where everyone has an obligation to be civil and decent to each other and listen to opposing views. It is a fragile silicon bubble. In cyberspace, the person at the other end of the conversation is only a series of electronic impulses – which means that to him or to her, that is all you are, too: a set of data bits, floating in something that tries to pass for a place but is really nowhere at all."

And that is truly symbolic of the VIRTUAL REALITY of this physical world we humans live in. This life is little more than nothing spinning extremely fast, no matter how important one thinks his or her life is, it is not **ACTUAL REALITY**. From an Old Testament book, *"Vanity of vanities, saith the preacher; all is vanity."* (Ecclesiastes 12:8) We can live in this physical (carnal) world and not be of it, we can see through its illusion and the time-wrapped mortality of its VIRTUAL REALITY, and seek God's will, fight the battle of faith, deny our selves and follow Christ into that immortal **ACTUAL REALITY** of GOD'S. The war is within, between our carnal mind and our spiritual mind. Everything, from some forms of virtual reality of cyberspace to false 'logical' doctrines such as 'thorough-going' (i.e. extremist), Darwinian views, can all be used as tools by Satan to confuse humans in an attempt to destroy the faith of some in Almighty God. This does not mean that cyberspace or evolution (as examples) are bad, but that they can, at times, confuse and obfuscate the real issues.

If one relies upon reason to make sense of his or her world, one still may not have to see it or touch it to believe in its reality. For example, one may accept, as factual reality, statements of mathematical proofs or claims of science, especially in physics, mathematics or chemistry. As long as they can be 'proven' or established by the scientific method. Thus, one could probably accept carbon dating as a means of determining the age of fossils, bones and archaeological claims. One may accept a sedimentological theory insofar as it pertains to claims made to determine when certain events happened: beginnings, ending and sequences in anthropological contexts. One may claim to be entirely 'scientific' and totally refute anything involving reliance upon 'faith'. Yet that person may accept the claims made by 'thorough-going', Darwinian extremists, even in their 'further-out' reaches, as 'scientific'. A person with such a belief system may even so, be open to further consideration in a discussion that God could have used a form of evolution in His plans, and thus accept that there may be a Master Mind, a Creator, behind the universe – as we know it.

The Bible could very well be, in part, symbolic and our ancestors perhaps do reach back millions of years. The Bible indicates that God has dealt with man in different ways, over recorded history. Theologians refer to these different periods as 'dispensations'; however, in this discussion, the 'dispensations' would reach further into the past by eons than theologians have attributed to them. As I see it, God could be developing a creature that will evolve into a spiritual being from a physical (carnal) animal. In the recorded history of man, there does not seem to have been much progress made in that direction thus far. The human, by and large, tends to be an animal and not a spiritual being. Those with the largest 'egos', that is, having the most self-seeking and self-aggrandizing natures, when combined with natural gifts of mental or physical prowess or of a charismatic personality, are the most worldly successful even when these gifts are used ruthlessly and relentlessly. These humans, more often than not, garner the most adulation and emulation from others and are usually considered heroes. However, no matter how worldly successful they have been, eventually they die; and when they die, they could die as animals. (That is, carnal or worldly success does not insure spiritual 'success' hereafter.)

A 'Darwinian' who limits himself to human logic and experience would be hard put to explain from whence did the sea and the land arise, to say nothing of the first living cell and the 'magical' transformations from that amoeba to the myriad of complex creatures that pervade our planet; not to mention the planetary systems and the starry universe. To say it all began as an accident and arose from nothing is to exhibit a credulity that makes Christian faith pale in contrast to such cullibility, such naivete as to be pathetic sophistry, worthy of a true zealot. This type of 'thinking' is parochial and nihilistic, which ironically results in revealing the existence of a mind that denies reality because of the inability to grasp any system of thought or cognition beyond its own logic or experience. If such a Darwinian can limit this type of reasoning, open up his mind and grant the concession that there has to be a 'master mind' behind this universe and, therefore, there may well be a reason for existence, wonderful!

Posit God and consider both the Judaic God and His Ten Commandments and the Christian God and His Son's proclamations of: *"And thou shalt love the Lord thy God with all thy heart, and with all thy soul, and with all thy mind, and with all thy strength: this is the first commandment. And the second is like, namely this, Thou shalt love thy neighbour as thyself. There is none other commandment greater than these."* (Mark 12:30-31) This creed, if followed, would make a paradise on earth. Yet, we have not even approached applying these very reasonable truths to our daily living. No society has. In fact, if one were to look at the basic instructions for a 'good' society anywhere in the world, in any culture, be they religious or philosophical, one would not find any group putting them into consistent and inclusive practice. Isn't it odd, that human beings, with their marvelous brain and modern advances and advantages, have not formed a utopia at any time any where on earth, in recorded history?!?

There is a reason for this, in my belief. Humanity has been infected with a 'virus' handed down generation after generation from the first man, Adam (symbolic or historical, it really doesn't matter – for the sake of discussion). In other words, we all have a fatal gene from Adam's failure. Certainly, there is something at work in our world that defeats reason, common sense and happiness.

That force is evil, which is called sin and is man's susceptibility to Satan, who is out to destroy God's crowning creation – man. Satan works through man's natural (or carnal) self; it separates him from God. Until humans deny self and follow the life and truth of Jesus Christ, they will continue to be infected with greed, lust, hate and all the other vices revealed throughout human history. Man cannot overcome this by effort or intelligence, but only by surrender to Christ and the Holy Spirit, and this is on an individual transition from being an animal to 'becoming' a spiritual being. *". . . Not by might, nor by power, but by My Spirit, saith the Lord of hosts."* (Zechariah 4:6)

If you are a believer in evolution, it doesn't preclude your ability to believe in a creator; if you are not an extremist or a Darwinian zealot, and certainly, if you have read this far in this book, and if much of it makes sense to you, then, as I read the Bible, you have been 'called'* and it is your further spiritual growth that will determine whether you will be 'chosen' or not. The theme of this book reflects my belief that the difference between being 'called' and being 'chosen' is the difference between a 'believer' and a 'saint', as described in previous chapters. (I believe both are 'saved').[See page 182.]

We are in a mortal combat, and the enemy is within ourselves; it is our natural (carnal) mind. If we are not to die as animals, if we are to experience a new life, everlasting with joy and love beyond anything we could ever have even dreamed, then we must become Spiritually minded. This can only happen when we turn to Christ and rely on the Holy Spirit as set forth in the New Testament.

The enemy is the self, the savior is Christ, and to be with God is joy, peace, love and life.

*See page 20.

Chapter 20
Subtle Subversion of Self

Identity is who you are and results from your experiences, perceptions and feedback from important others, such as parents, peers, teachers and, most importantly, from God. Carnal self, on the other hand, is an interloper who usurps the individual's identity with God and becomes an autonomously functioning mode of behavior and thinking. This is directed by Satan to varying degrees, as 'necessitated' by the individual's struggle to become united with, or to return to, God (i.e., the more one strives to become united with God, the more Satan attempts to introduce doubt and to destroy one's relationship with God). Self is a construct and an artifact of Adam's fall. It is false and the basis of VIRTUAL REALITY.

Carnal self is the 'bad' part of individual identity; it is not the same as a person's identity. As stated in prior chapters, self inserts itself between the unique individual and God; it is like a rotten spot in his or her identity. It is a powerful weapon in the cosmic struggle going on for the soul of man and it is used by Satan. That is why, as in our Lord's words, "*. . . If any man will come after Me, let him deny himself, and take up his cross, and follow Me.*" (Matthew 16:24) Denying the self is not the same as losing your identity. It is removing the separation from God – and it takes time; it seems to be a growth and learning experience, and brings into the core of your being, peace and love and all the fruits of the Spirit. You may continue to be as you are or you may become an even better athlete, executive, mother, worker, professor, painter or whatever part you play on the stage of the world; but that is not to say more worldly successful. **Your joy will be greater and you will be different.** Carnal self and self are one and the same. Self not only blocks awareness of God but also causes confusion in the identity. Self is false to the 'nth' degree and is Satan's portal to the person, and it is with this 'trump ace' that he deceives man and mankind.

Psychology is working in ignorance of that fact if it fosters the self and, thereby, places the individual in a progressively worsening situation. The psychologist's emphasis upon self-esteem and self-worth, for example, just strengthens this autonomous part of the individual that is so subtle and destructive. These are not seen as in the same family as self-consciousness, self-centeredness, self-aggrandizement or selfishness; however, they are all from the same source and eventually bear bitter fruit to others and always to the individual thus controlled.

People think of themselves in a self-conscious sense, to varying degrees. Many people are not overly concerned with themselves but, unfortunately, most of these 'normal' people do not dwell on God or His purposes and wishes for them, either. They, therefore, not only fall short of what He requires, but ironically fall short of their own uniqueness and ability. In fact, many of these 'normal' people (or 'average' people) may fall into the class of those who either don't care about, or don't know that they don't know, the role 'self' plays in their own destiny. Then there are others, some of whom are overly concerned with themselves (not in a selfish way), who are often painfully self-conscious. I have a feeling that these are among the ones in whom Satan is most active in trying to derail or deter and destroy, since they may have the potential to be 'saints' and/or workers for God and His purposes. (Because they make life so difficult for themselves and tend to be so unhappy, they are motivated to think more deeply than people who are self-satisfied and happy with the status quo of their own personality.) I believe there are also a group of people who cannot or will not love others – in a selfless way – and in fact, who are often the most destructive to their own families or loved ones.

Concerning the role that 'self' plays in one's ultimate destiny, many people can be grouped in the following categories:

1) those who don't care;
2) those who don't know;
3) those who don't know that they don't know, but think they do;

4) those who are engaged or committed to self;
5) those who are struggling with self;
6) those who are trying to give up or deny self and are attempting to follow Christ.

This last category is a tricky one in that some people might class themselves in this group; whereas, in fact, they may actually be self-deceived, often touting honorable or even Christian ends, but using (intentionally or unknowingly) destructive means. The last two categories are most apt to yield true Christians. In the first three categories reside those who are unaware of self, even when it predominates. For example, a person who is obviously extremely self-centered and selfish, yet denies this fact or even be unaware of it – and be impervious to having his attention called to it. The fourth group contains the most ruthless as well as most of the manipulators and 'users'. We all have many, many parts to our identity that make us unique individuals. However, we must strive to have God at the core of our being, and then we begin to become Spiritually minded and start to become free of our carnal self. As you can see from the two previous paragraphs, there are many crossovers between groups and much diversity within groups (another reason not to be judgmental).

Carnal self is the vulnerable part of you, it is the gateway for the power of evil – the broad path that leads to destruction. *"Enter ye in at the strait gate: for wide is the gate, and broad is the way, that leadeth to destruction, and many there be which go in thereat: Because strait is the gate, and narrow is the way, which leadeth unto life, and few there be that find it."* (Matthew 7:13-14) After you have 'accepted' Christ and begin to allow God's gift of faith into your soul and seek the guidance of the Holy Spirit, life's experiences do not often reassure you. You are forced into relying upon hope because of the very nature of faith. *"Now faith is the substance of things hoped for, the evidence of things not seen."* (Hebrews 11:1) God demands faith, *"But without faith it is impossible to please Him: for he that cometh to God must believe that He is, and that He is a rewarder of them that diligently seek Him."* (Hebrews 11:6) Thus, hope plays such a major role in maintaining and nourishing our faith. *"And hope maketh not ashamed; because the love of God is shed abroad in our hearts by the Holy Ghost which is given unto us."* (Romans 5:5) The love of God begins to soften our hearts and open us up to real hope that He loves us, i.e., we *feel* that love – perhaps only momentarily – but it is there, and we begin to believe it. As we continue to hope and grow in faith, our self (I believe, in proportion to our growth in faith) starts to diminish, and a peace takes up residence within us. We begin to relax and become calmer, losing our contentiousness and negativism.

Joy makes its visits with us more and more. But then come times when we have relapses and it may seem as if we are no longer aware of these wonderful spiritual gifts and we are back struggling with our selves. This, to me, is normal; it is a growth process and a learning experience and we must, must rely on hope. As our faith grows stronger and God's love becomes more of a resident within us, we feel love toward God more and more and begin to be able to be loving toward others in the sense of 'agape' (spontaneous, self-giving love expressed freely without calculation of cost or gain to the giver or merit on the part of the receiver). [Webster's Third New International Dictionary]

After all, our faith may be tried, but our sufferings and dark nights will not compare to what Christ endured. Hold in mind that it is Satan trying to break us down, make us lose hope, destroy our faith. *"Blessed is the man that endureth temptation: for when he is tried, he shall receive the crown of life, which the Lord hath promised to them that love Him. Let no man say when he is tempted, I am tempted of God: for God cannot be tempted with evil, neither tempteth He any man: But every man is tempted, when he is drawn away of his own lust, and enticed. Then when lust hath conceived, it bringeth forth sin: and sin, when it is finished, bringeth forth death."* (James 1:12-15) If a person tries to be morally and ethically clean without a spiritual foundation, he may become a worse person or even evil. (See Matthew 12:43-45.)

This temptation comes from Satan and happens when we turn

to our carnal selves. We will not let our carnal self have its way with us, but rather turn toward God and become increasingly Spiritually minded. Sin will not have its way with us because we will reject the carnal self and turn to Christ. So, we must hold on to our faith through hope, and abandon our dying carnal selves.

If we have survived an accident or ordeal, especially when others haven't, it is important we realize that God has delivered us – even though we know not why we were spared when someone else wasn't. We do not know God's ways; we need not think we were granted life because we deserved it or because we were less a sinner than someone who succumbed. We cannot judge others and we do not know why we made it but it is important to thank God and to 'know' that He has His reasons, and just turn to Him in acceptance and thanksgiving. We may have work left to do. *"Be still, and know that I am God. . ."* (Psalm 46:10) Perhaps this could be paraphrased, Be quiet and experience Me.

Carnal self is a linking (a concatenation) with evil, the devil. We are, each of us, unique individuals with different identities that grow and change; i.e., identity is dynamic but self inserts itself as a false part of identity and makes for pride, greed and other vices and attempts to rule the identity. It is a separating force from God and from others in its censuring activities. Even Christ said, *"I can of mine own self do nothing: as I hear, I judge: and my judgment is just; because I seek not mine own will, but the will of the Father which hath sent Me."* (John 5:30) There is one Self that is good; all other selves are counterfeit and of the devil. That 'only' and valid 'Self' is God: *"And now, O Father, glorify Thou Me with Thine own Self with the glory which I had with thee before the world was."* (John 17:5) **So we turn from carnal self, which is of the devil, become Spiritually minded and take on the only good and genuine Self, which is God. We aim toward and, eventually, become one with God. His Self is at the core of our being.**

We need not complicate this very basic issue with straining at a semantics 'gnat'. Of course, in everyday speech, we use self, myself, himself, themselves, etc. Although one may continue to refer to self-esteem, self-confidence, self-consciousness, it is of very great importance to realize more and more that it is this 'self' which is the main culprit in one's estrangement from God, and we must reorient so that God becomes our center. Self-centeredness and self-consciousness are to be overcome just as much as self-aggrandizement and self-seeking. In the New Testament, we are urged to 'overcome' (see Revelations 2:7, Revelations 2:11, and Revelations 21:7). Overcome what? (see 1 John 5:4-5). We need to overcome the 'world' of carnality, materialism and sensuality, which is all just a temporary virtuality that revolves around the self.

Chapter 21
Wantonness of Will

God and Christ are one, and they invite us to be one with them. There is One Will – God's, and One Self – God. Self-love, free love, self-will, free will and will-full are all branches of the same tree, whose trunk is the idolatry of man and whose roots reach deep into our past into the garden of Eden that bore the fruit of which Adam and Eve partook.

The will is a human construct and only exists in VIRTUAL REALITY. We tout 'free will' as if it were something that men should die for and that we humans should be proud of, that it is a wonderful gift that God gave us, that He gave us Free Will! He did not give us free will; in fact, free will is not mentioned in the Bible except for freewill offerings. God gave us freedom to choose His will, but the concept of free will is as unchristian as free love. Free will is exalting yourself above God, supplanting God with yourself. Free will is one way in which Satan confuses humans; it is the technique of the 'big lie'. Man has had freedom to choose and, since Adam, he has almost always, as a group, chosen wrong! However, there is only one Will, and that is God's Will.

Newt Gingrich and the so called 'Republican Revolution' are 1) pushing what our founding fathers put forth and 2) emphasizing the technological advances of the computer age and the information highway. There needs to be caution exercised, because the founding fathers were fallible humans. It is not self-evident that all men are created equal and even that our Creator endowed us with unalienable rights, such as life and liberty. I believe equality, life and liberty would only apply spiritually and not in this world. I certainly do not know where they perceived that right in regards to the pursuit of happiness. Many Americans interpret that phrase today as meaning sensual and physical pleasures or hedonism. To pursue happiness is far different than to **be** happy. The Bible says, *"Happy is he that hath the God of Jacob for his help, whose hope is in the Lord his God: Which made heaven, and earth, the sea,* *and all that therein is: which keepeth truth forever:"* (Psalm 146:5-6) *"Happy is the man that feareth always: but he that hardeneth his heart shall fall into mischief."* (Proverb 28:14) *"If ye be reproached for the name of Christ, happy are ye; for the spirit of glory and of God resteth upon you: on their part He is evil spoken of, but on your part He is glorified."* (1 Peter 4:14) Happiness, in the sense of a deep abiding joy, is a spiritual gift.

Furthermore, the current stress on and hope that rests in technology is a two-edged sword. Even George Washington in his 'farewell address' gave stern warnings against not being on guard against small clever minorities that attempt to change or control the government. Today, in the era of huge 'takeovers' in business, establishing monopolies in communication, entertainment and the media; as well as in industry and banking, we must be careful to stay in touch with our God. Excessive control, power and wealth does put into the hands of the few, the possibility of the domination over the many. We, as Christians, are to be obedient to authority, but we must take care not to get caught up with viewing science and the pursuit of 'happiness' as the purpose of human life.

Will gets intricately interwoven with self. We have freedom in America (political, social, etc.) up to the point of violent or forbidden intrusion upon another. Even then, we have the ability or opportunity to do those things – but not permission to, and if we violate someone else's freedom, we can pay for it by the loss of our own freedom. However, freedom is not to be confused with free will, which is a non-sequitor (does not follow). Adam and Eve, when they were given freedom, mistook that for free will and found out to their sorrow (and ours) that they did not have free will; that they had freedom to choose or to reject God's will ('do not eat of the fruit of the tree of the knowledge of good and evil'). It is my belief that we were created without a self and without a will, and as Christians we must get back to that stage. Listen to Jesus' words again. *". . . Whosoever will come after Me, let him deny himself. . ."* (Mark 8:34) *"I can of Mine own self do nothing: as I hear, I judge: and My judgment is just; because I seek not*

Mine own will, but the will of the Father which hath sent Me." (John 5:30) *"Thy kingdom come. Thy will be done in earth, as it is in heaven."* (Matthew 6:10) *"Not every one that saith unto Me, Lord, Lord, shall enter into the kingdom of heaven; but he that doeth the will of My Father which is in heaven."* (Matthew 7:21) *"But chiefly them that walk after the flesh in the lust of uncleanness, and despise government. Presumptuous are they, self-willed, they are not afraid to speak evil of dignities."* (2 Peter 2:10)

We must become one with God and with the Lord and, in order to do this, we must get rid of that false illusion of the existence of 'self' and, furthermore, we must seek the Will of God and overcome the 'big lie' of having a 'free' will. We are free to deny God and live in a world, 'made' by man and Satan – a land of dreams (at bottom, nightmares), that is as a 'blade of grass' in a desert that, in a moment, is withered and destroyed by the sun. If so, we are carnal minded and no more than animals, and will die in an ignoble and ignominious mortality.

This does not have to be our fate, but we must put God at our core and do so by constantly seeking the Holy Spirit's guidance through faith in Jesus Christ, and this has to be sustained by hope in the early stages until our faith has been nourished enough that we 'know' that God is, and that He is good and that He loves us. Then, we see His presence in each moment of our lives and feel Him in our lives; this occurs only through faith, which He gives to us to accept and use.

It is wonderful as we gradually grow in awareness of His presence and His love, and we find peace and joy as we 'blend' with Him. Just as Christ said, *"I and My Father are one."* (John 10:30) *"And now I am no more in the world, but these are in the world, and I come to Thee. Holy Father, keep through Thine Own name those whom Thou hast given Me, that they may be one, as We are."* (John 17:11) *"That they all may be one; as Thou, Father, art in Me, and I in Thee, that they also may be one in Us: that the world may believe that Thou hast sent Me."* (John 17:21) *"And the glory which Thou gavest Me I have given them; that they may be one, even as We are One:"* (John 17:22) *"I in them, and Thou in Me, that they may be made perfect in one; and that the world may know that Thou hast sent Me, and hast loved them, as Thou hast loved Me."* (John 17:23)

Just grasp the import of that! It is astounding. Think about it a while. Really, just lay the book down and dwell on this; meditate on these passages. Nothing more wonderful could possibly happen to us than that we be one with God, our Creator and Father, and with Jesus Christ – His son, our Redeemer and Saviour.

When God says, *"And God said unto Moses, **I AM THAT I AM:** and He said, Thus shalt thou say unto the children of Israel, I Am hath sent me unto you."* (Exodus 3:14) This name, **I AM**, indicates to me that He was, He is, He will be. In other words, He just **is**. The **I AM**, is outside of time; it supersedes time. Time is, I believe, an artifact of VIRTUAL REALITY and will not exist in **ACTUAL REALITY**; by definition, eternity and immortality are timeless. **I AM** conveys more than I always have been and I always will be; somehow **HE is**. It conveys His constant and perpetual instant immediacy.

Jesus said, *"And He said unto him, Why callest thou Me good? there is none good but one, that is, God: but if thou wilt enter into life, keep the commandments."*(Matthew 19:17) What is good? What is the difference between good and evil? What is sin?

Sin is missing the mark, i.e., failing the goal (failing to be who you **are**), and the bottom line is that it is failing to be one with **'I AM'**. In other words, not being one with God and Christ, not being who you **are** (created in God's image). It is remaining in Satan's VIRTUAL REALITY, his counterfeit world. This happens when you do not enter God's ***ACTUAL REALITY*** through faith and striving to be receptive, attentive and obedient to the Holy Ghost. Sin is not what Satan would have us believe, it is not being 'naughty' or 'dirty' or 'bad'. It is being separated from God and Christ and the Holy Spirit; it is failure to use hope to nourish the faith that God has offered you. It is being separated from God by your choice! The devil confuses us and misleads us by having us focus on petty things: sex, lust, money; that is, acts and behavior which, while they are not good, make us overlook the real issues of self and willfulness. Instead, we focus our attention on the symptoms, the physical, the natural, which are mortal and will vanish, as will those caught up in Satan's VIRTUAL REALITY. In other words, Satan often utilizes a technique that is much the same as telling someone to stand in the corner and not think of a pink elephant for five minutes! How deceptive and cunning is the devil. In fact, we can only avoid his wiles and his pitfalls, set for us, by turning to the Lord.

Jesus says through St. Paul via the Holy Ghost, *"Finally, brethren, whatsoever things are true, whatsoever things are honest, whatsoever things are just, whatsoever things are pure, whatsoever things are lovely, whatsoever things are of good report; if there be any virtue, and if there be any praise, think on these things."* (Philippians 4:8) Dwell on the good and the positive, reject the negative, the pessimistic, the bad and gossip. This is not only good for the spirit, but it is excellent advice for daily living in ones' career and duties. One of the worst things one can do is to 'rehearse' repetitiously what to say or to engage in 'what if' thinking, that is, to focus on the negative and keep rehashing it. That begins a cycle of worry, anxiety and tension.

God is good, perfect and one. *"There is no fear in love; but perfect love casteth out fear: because fear hath torment. He that feareth is not made perfect in love."* (John 4:18) *"I in them, and Thou in Me, that they may be made perfect in one; and that the world may know that Thou hast sent Me, and hast loved them, as Thou hast loved Me."* (John 17:23)

The prophets of old, the holy men of God: Elijah, Elisha, Samuel, Isaiah, Jeremiah, et al, were not ostentatious in lifestyle, but were humble, devout humans; in a sense, as compared with the kings and warriors, they were the unsung heroes of the nation. Just so must the Christian be unprepossessing in manner and in life. *"For ye are dead, and your life is hid with Christ in God."* (Colossians 3:3) *"And be not conformed to this world: but be ye transformed by the renewing of your mind, that ye may prove what is that good, and acceptable, and perfect, will of God."* (Romans 12:2) The puzzling act of Jesus concerning the fig tree (see Mark 11:12-14), means to me that the Christian must be fruitful in season and out (see 2 Timothy 4:2). It also illustrates that we must accept the Bible and lay aside those portions we do not understand until God decides it is important or necessary to enlighten us on some particular passage that has been obscure or puzzling. In fact, I have found it not to be unusual that those passages which troubled me most, eventually came to be the most meaningful, years later! The difference between good and evil is the difference between immortality and mortality. It is the difference between God's ***ACTUAL REALITY*** and Satan's VIRTUAL REALITY, the genuine and the counterfeit.

There is no Will but the Will of God. *"But as many as received Him, to them gave He power to become the sons of God, even to them that believe on His name: Which were born, not of blood, nor of the will of the flesh, nor of the will of man, but of God."* (John 1:12-13)

Even Jesus Christ, the Son of God, said, in many different ways, there is One Self and One Will – **God's**. As one example, *"I can of Mine Own Self do nothing: as I hear, I judge: and My judgment is just; because I seek not Mine Own will, but the Will of the Father which hath sent Me."* (John 5:30)

A Prayer of Striving to Be

I will wait on the Lord; I can do nothing of myself.
I will allow the love of God, which passes all understanding, to become a constant presence within me.
I will not let my 'impotence' make me doubt His presence; He will have His way with me, I will just wait and be.
I will let my actions as well as my thoughts be peaceful, trusting and non-contentious.
I am a receptor; I am to be as the Lord commands.
If there is to be action, God will direct and enable me.
If there is to be a response or words, God will give them to me.
If there are to be thoughts, God will inspire me.
I will be waitful and alert, but I will have patience.
I will meditate on the Bible.
I will do productive work according to the skills given to me.
I will worship the Lord in my inner temple and share my joy with others as the opportunities arise.
I will live in joy, peace, love, hope, and faith.
I will let this become who I be in God.

Chapter 22
End of Time

The transformation of essence into existence and on-going perfection has been accomplished, in human form, despite chaos. All the 'sea' of humanity could not produce one perfect human to survive time and death until God 'birthed' Himself.

Jesus Christ was, is and always shall be one with God, and any human living today can be one with Them. He came back from death and, in so doing, not only conquered death for us, but provides us with freedom from the fear of death. One confirmation that you have been turning to the Holy Spirit and have been asking Him and allowing Him to be active within you is that you do not fear death. Death is meaningless; it is but a transfer from our time-trapped world into the eternal world of God. Time is as meaningless as death; evil and troubles will no longer exist. They 'exist' now in our time-trapped earth, but they no longer control or intimidate us, once we are in Christ, having rejected the 'self's' usurpation of God and His Will.

Both Jesus Christ's Virgin Birth and His death and Resurrection are essential to our belief and life as Christians.

His Virgin Birth indicates that He was not merely of human form, but He was God Who visited us in our form and led our type of human life, *"And the Word was made flesh, and dwelt among us, (and we beheld His glory, the glory as of the only begotten of the Father,) full of grace and truth."* (John 1:14); *"That which was from the beginning, which we have heard, which we have seen with our eyes, which we have looked upon, and our hands have handled, of the Word of life;"* (1 John 1:1) But He was without sin, was sinless before birth and after birth, unlike we humans. Several efforts were made by Satan (and man) to tempt Him, but Jesus was not tempted and did not yield. However, the first time man and woman were tempted, they lusted and sinned. *"So God created man in His own image, in the image of God created He him; male and female created He them."* (Genesis 1:27) *"And the serpent said unto the woman, Ye shall not surely die: For God doth know that in the day ye eat thereof, then your eyes shall be opened, and ye shall be as gods, knowing good and evil."* (Genesis 3:4-5) Man was lied to by Satan who told him that he was created able to become 'as gods', which he lusted for, which led to sinning in that he disobeyed God and tried to go beyond what God created him to be and do. *"And God said, Let Us make man in Our image, after Our likeness: and let them have dominion over the fish of the sea, and over the fowl of the air, and over the cattle, and over all the earth, and over every creeping thing that creepeth on the earth."* (Genesis 1:26) That apparently was not enough – mankind wanted to be 'as gods'. And he continues to disobey and lust for becoming 'as gods', to this day! Yet we can become one with God with His blessing, through Jesus Christ. It seems that that is not 'good' enough for most men and women today, just as it was not enough for mankind in the millenniums since Eden. It is as if most of mankind would rather believe they are descended from monkeys than from God!?!

His death and Resurrection reveals to us that He conquered death, the grave and Satan and, thus, frees us from the fear of death and the desperation to 'get it all' now, as if this life and this world were the end. *"Forasmuch then as the children are partakers of flesh and blood, He also Himself likewise took part of the same; that through death He might destroy him that had the power of death, that is, the devil; and deliver them who through fear of death were all their lifetime subject to bondage."* (Hebrews 2:14-15) *"For the law of the Spirit of life in Christ Jesus hath made me free from the law of sin and death."* (Romans 8:2) What freedom this gives us. It is (depending on how important it is to us) as St. Paul states, *"For none of us liveth to himself, and no man dieth to himself. For whether we live, we live unto the Lord; and whether we die, we die unto the Lord: whether we live therefore, or die, we are the Lord's. For to this end Christ both died, and rose, and revived, that He might be Lord both of the dead and living."* (Romans 14:7-9) He had to die and come back from death to show us His power over

Satan and death in order to free us from compromising fear. Enoch and Elijah were taken up bodily into heaven and never died, but Jesus did die, was buried and rose again in a victory over the grave and over death. Yet today, humans continue to have the propensity to deny the Truth and to be Free as God intended. *"Ever learning, and never able to come to the knowledge of the truth."* (2 Timothy 3:7)

Time disappears forever when death, with resurrection to immortality, occurs – by definition. Thus, what Christ's Virgin Birth, death and Resurrection demonstrates is God's love for us and how He wants us to live and eventually **be**.

It might be helpful to view the Bible analogous to a computer manual that is worded in an operating system language (like Windows '95) that is more comprehensible to us than machine language such as FORTRAN; whereas in the Bible, God is communicating to us in a language we can understand. So, He conveys to us the concept of time by stating that the world was created in a 'day' (Genesis 2:4). In another place He states that a 'day' is with the Lord as a thousand years and a thousand years as a day (2 Peter 3:8). I am of the belief that time is a concept that is an artifact of man's downfall and only exists in our transformation period on earth, wherein we become one with God or perhaps, more accurately, prepare to become one with God and to reside in His presence, immortally.

I believe that our 'animal' natures are not due to evolution but come from Satan's initial, ongoing and constant efforts to separate every human being from God and to set him against God, in an effort to destroy every human he can. It is my understanding that the Moslem religion acknowledges Christ's Virgin Birth, but denies that He was ever crucified or killed; rather, they believe He was taken up into heaven bodily as were Elijah and Enoch. If my understanding of this facet of the Moslem religion is accurate, I am sure they are sincere in this belief and I do not intend to disparage Muslims, but I do feel that this is a subtle chipping away at Christianity (whether inadvertent or not is irrelevant), and it could undermine a basic tenet of our faith.* It is so vital that we do not give up what has been revealed to us. This does not mean that we should judge or condemn the Moslems; they have a right to their belief and faith. We, as Christians, are to live in peace and goodwill with all men. Thus, neither do Christians condemn nor 'blame' Jews for the death of Christ. After all, Christ forgave them and, furthermore, they do not believe the Messiah has yet come. This is their faith in which they are sincere and have a right to believe as they will. The positions put forth throughout this book are from a Christian viewpoint and, hopefully, will not be taken in judgment of other religions simply because we have a right to profess our faith, as do others.

God challenges us to prove His presence and His truths as Jesus propounded them. In so doing, He reveals that we are '**receptors**'. *"And be not conformed to this world: but be ye transformed by the renewing of your mind, that ye may prove what is that good, and acceptable, and perfect, will of God."* (Romans 12:2) Further to this point, *"Examine yourselves, whether ye be in the faith; prove your own selves. Know ye not your own selves, how that Jesus Christ is in you, except ye be reprobates?"* (2 Corinthians 13:5) And, *"But let every man prove his own work, and then shall he have rejoicing in himself alone, and not in another."* (Galations 6:4) *"Prove all things; hold fast that which is good."* (1 Thessalonians 5:21)

A dramatic example of how we are '**receptors**' is illustrated in the 16th chapter of Matthew involving Saint Peter. *"He saith unto them, But whom say ye that I am? And Simon Peter answered and said, Thou art the Christ, the Son of the living God. And Jesus answered and said unto him, Blessed art thou, Simon Bar-jona: for flesh and blood hath not revealed it unto thee, but My Father which is in heaven."* Matthew 16:15-17) Then, a few verses later, *"From that time forth began Jesus to shew unto His disciples, how that He must go unto Jerusalem, and suffer many things of the elders and chief priests and scribes, and be killed, and be raised again the third day. Then Peter took Him, and began to rebuke*

Him, saying, Be it far from Thee, Lord: this shall not be unto Thee. But He turned, and said unto Peter, Get thee behind Me, Satan: thou art an offense unto Me: for thou savourest not the things that be of God, but those that be of men." (Matthew 16:21-23) Here we see Peter receiving a message from God first, followed shortly by a message from Satan. What this further shows is how much of a learning process it is to be in tune with the Holy Spirit, rather than with Satan, and to be able to distinguish. Even Peter, at that point, did not distinguish; therefore, we can all take heart and be patient with ourselves. I believe it is essential that our desire and motivation be increasingly toward giving up our 'self' and our 'will', and seeking the guidance and resultant 'fruit' of the Holy Spirit: joy, peace, patience, faith and love, to name some of them.

There is no question in my mind that Jesus knew, in advance, that this sequence of events was going to happen with Peter and yet, before He chastised Peter, He gave him the 'keys of the kingdom'. *"And I say also unto thee, That thou art Peter, and upon this rock I will build My church; and the gates of hell shall not prevail against it. And I will give unto thee the keys of the kingdom of heaven: and whatsoever thou shalt bind on earth shall be bound in heaven: and whatsoever thou shalt loose on earth shall be loosed in heaven."* (Matthew 16:18-19) It appears to me this was a teaching exercise not just for the benefit of the disciples, but for us also. We will make mistakes and error in judgment as **receptors**, but God is patient and forgiving and, even in our bumbling and stumbling, we will receive 'fruit' from the Holy Spirit. We will gradually learn when He is directing us and when some urge or impulse is from the devil.

Because it is all a matter of faith, and because most of us, who do have faith, have such a weak faith, that all guidance is subtle or indirect and there is ample opportunity for doubt, which Satan delights in and makes the most of, we must nurture hope all the more. It is a constant battle for faith and of faith. It appears that perhaps it is this constant battle for faith, and demonstrating it in our lives, that God requires of us, that is the only way most of us can please God. Faith means believing in Jesus Christ, and believing in what He tells us about God and His love for us, and in the way that God wants us to live and **be**.

It is important and helpful to keep in mind that our faith must be increasingly a living faith; it must become the central core of our lives. *"But what think ye? A certain man had two sons; and he came to the first, and said, Son, go work to day in my vineyard. He answered and said, I will not: but afterward he repented, and went. And he came to the second, and said likewise. And he answered and said, I go, sir: and went not. Whether of them twain did the will of his father? They say unto Him, The first. Jesus saith unto them, Verily I say unto you, That the publicans and the harlots go into the kingdom of God before you."* (Matthew 21:28-31) [Jesus refers here to the chief priests and the elders, in the temple.]

Sacrifice in the Old Testament meant to slay or slaughter, that is, to kill an animal and to burn its body on an altar as a burnt offering to the Lord. Genesis 22:1-18 is a fore-shadowing of Jesus Christ's sacrifice where-in He was crucified and died, only to defeat death and Satan and rise up into life immortal and, in so doing, atone for the sins of all mankind. Today, the only sacrifice we need to make is to deny 'self' and to live as He taught us which, in effect, is to 'die' to this world. Thus, ironically, we give up worldly pleasures of the 'self' and willfulness in order to survive this world of woes, injustices and time, entering into immortality and paradise. To sum it up, we survive by surrendering to the love of God.

*Jesus is the Christ; He is the Messiah. He is unique. He was God manifesting Himself in human form with human limitations, except that He was sinless, and His miracles we could replicate were we also sinless. He became one of us to show how much He loved us and how He wanted us to live, only with and as God could such a dramatization ever occur. God is the only One we worship. Polytheism does not exist. God's Holy Spirit communicates with us Spiritually. God is One and we can become one with Him. Furthermore, only He knows who are saints and who are believers. We may not know until the Day of Judgement. But all who are chosen will become part of the Body of Christ, each an immortal part of God's creation. We are all different and yet equally loved by God, IF we so choose to love and obey Him.

Chapter 23
Last Word

Christ calls us to action. We are to live His creed and, in so doing, we may begin to enter the Kingdom of God (**ACTUAL REALITY) now**, here in our earthly VIRTUAL REALITY. For example, when He says, *". . .If ye continue in My word, then are ye My disciples indeed; And ye shall know the truth, and the truth shall make you free."* (John 8: 31-32) His word is love – of God, for God and toward man. In perfect love, there is neither fear nor torment. To know the truth and to experience it is to be free. To be truthful and to be loving is to possess a peace that surpasses all comprehension, for then you are one with God and Jesus Christ.

BUT! Jesus asks much of us when He says, *"continue in My word."* He is asking of us more than we can possibly do, alone. For example, He says *"Be ye therefore perfect, even as your Father in heaven is perfect."* (Matthew 5:48) If we cannot do that, why then did He say that? He said that and He said many other things, such as, *"But I say unto you, That ye resist not evil: but whosoever shall smite thee on thy right cheek, turn to him the other also."* (Matthew 5:39); and further, *"But I say unto you, Love your enemies, bless them that curse you, do good to them that hate you, and pray for them which despitefully use you, and persecute you."* (Matthew 5:44) Can you do that consistently and without limit? No? Why then did Christ command that? Do any Christians you know (even after they have professed belief in the Bible, in Christ and feel that they are 'born again') follow His creed anymore than the Jews followed the ten commandments? What is the point of making us feel like failures in that we do not stop sinning – even after our 'conversion'? One more commandment from Christ, which is but one more among scores, *"Ye have heard that it was said by them of old time, Thou shalt not commit adultery: But I say unto you, That whosoever looketh on a woman to lust after her hath committed adultery with her already in his heart,"* (Matthew 5:27-28) What man can follow this immediately, consistently and permanently? Why all these seemingly 'impossible' commands? **BECAUSE,** I believe the point Jesus Christ is making is for us to realize that, without Him, we are lost and will be until we **DIE to self and become one with CHRIST!** (I also believe this is a growth process and one that is not completed before Christ returns) Lip service is not what Christ is all about. We need Christ and always will; without him, we are lost and lost forever unless and until we become one with Him and the Father (i.e., give up our 'selves') and do God's Will (we are to have one will, God's – not our own). If we do this, then we are a new creation in Christ. If we do not do this on earth in VIRTUAL REALITY, then our only hope of heaven is in dying in Christ. Either we die to ourselves and become one with Christ in the here and now, or we do so at our death, if it is in Christ.

This point is repeatedly made, as in the following case, *"And when He was gone forth into the way, there came one running, and kneeled to Him, and asked Him, Good Master, what shall I do that I may inherit eternal life? And Jesus said unto him, Why callest thou Me good? there is none good but one, that is, God.* Thou knowest the commandments, Do not commit adultery, Do not kill, Do not steal, Do not bear false witness, Defraud not, Honour thy father and mother. And he answered and said unto Him, Master, all these I have observed from my youth. Then Jesus beholding him loved him, and said unto him, One thing thou lackest: go thy way, sell whatsoever thou hast, and give to the poor, and thou shalt have treasure in heaven: and come, take up the cross, and follow Me. And he was sad at that saying, and went away grieved: for he had great possessions. And Jesus looked round about, and saith unto His disciples, How hardly shall they that have riches enter into the kingdom of God!"* (Mark 10:17-23)

(*There was and is an answer to that question, because **it was** a question; it was not just a statement. The answer was and is: Because Thou art God[†]. The man did not give that answer because he did not know that Jesus was and is God[†] and so, no matter how 'righteous' the man was, he was not worthy of the kingdom of God because humans are only worthy through Christ. Remember, Jesus has said: *"I and My Fa-*

ther are one." (John 10:30) One surely must admit that after trying to follow Christ's admonitions, one can only follow Jesus' commands insofar as one becomes one with Him, and this requires acceptance and understanding as well as a willingness, a wanting, to do this. We must acknowledge Christ as Son of God and keep trying to become one with Him. If we keep failing, it must increasingly result in our growing realization of how much we need Him, how indispensable He is and how impotent we are.)

This book is about five major personal goals to be achieved and lived in and through Jesus Christ:

1) faith in God;
2) hope for you and your loved ones;
3) love of God and toward man;
4) denying your-'self';
5) being led by the will of God.

It also urges a very basic national goal, regardless of skin color, sex, political position; and that is to provide for the comfort, dignity and wellbeing of children, elderly, helpless, sick, disabled, and handicapped. It is also important to promote parenting classes for couples wanting children, urging that only one spouse hold an income-producing job or work inside or outside the home until the youngest child has reached maturity.

A vital ingredient of Christianity is 'community', but one with no formal organization, no hierarchy of leaders. Community is about Christians helping one another, aiding those in need, and is comprised of families with or without physical proximity, but always spiritually compatible in Christ. (Refer to pages 17 and 20.)

Finally, one consistent theme and basic premise throughout the book is that this world of ours and our earthly life is VIRTUAL REALITY (artificial reality, counterfeit reality), and is a 'moment' of time encapsulated in the eternity of God's **ACTUAL REALITY**, and will disappear. So, in a way, I feel Mary Baker Eddy and her Christian Science was close to the truth saying evil does not exist. I disagree because, for some reason, we mortals do not understand this world of **time** and **evil** <u>does exist</u> for now and, until Christ returns, it is a cosmic struggle involving us that is beyond our comprehension.

It is not any particular economic or political system that is at fault, i.e., the cause of this world's evil (VIRTUAL REALITY). It is not democracy, communism, capital, labor, liberal or conservative; it is the **human heart**. For example, look at the feather bedding of the newspaper and railroad unions, on the part of labor. On the other hand, consider the obscene salaries and outrageous perquisites of some corporate executives, or the rampant rape and pillage of the land* and other natural resources on the part of capital. One could go on and on with examples of greed, waste and villainy in all human endeavors (professionals, craftsmen, tradesmen, artists, vendors, politicians), but the one common thread connecting them all is the human heart. The only salvation of any individual is to become Spiritually minded through Jesus Christ; and THAT constitutes the only and the ultimate **SURVIVAL** for all humans.

One of the more important things about faith is the necessity of relying on Christ. It does not depend upon us. We must rely on hope when we begin to doubt that God accepts us through Christ. Look at Peter ('the rock') who denied Christ three times before the cock crowed (Matthew 26:34), and Thomas, who doubted Jesus was Christ until he put his hands into His wounds (John 20:24-28). Yet, despite the denial and the doubt, Jesus made them disciples. He accepts us even though we have doubts about God or Christ at times, and especially if we doubt our acceptance by God. I further believe, as long as we go through Jesus Christ, God accepts us.

Another example was Peter on the stormy waters when Jesus asked him to walk on the water, *"But the ship was now in the midst of the sea, tossed with waves: for the wind was contrary. And in the fourth watch of the night Jesus went unto them, walking on the sea. And when the disciples saw Him walking on the sea, they were troubled, saying, It is a spirit; and they cried out for fear. But straightway Jesus spake unto them, saying, Be of good cheer; it is I; be not afraid. And Peter answered Him and said, Lord, if it be Thou, bid me come unto Thee on the water. And He said, Come.*

And when Peter was come down out of the ship, he walked on the water, to go to Jesus. But when he saw the wind boisterous, he was afraid; and beginning to sink, he cried, saying, Lord, save me. And immediately Jesus stretched forth His hand, and caught him, and said unto him, O thou of little faith, wherefore didst thou doubt?" (Matthew 14:24-31) This display of doubt was in himself, I believe, because when Jesus held out His hand, Peter was saved, and the doubt could have been about his-own worthiness, since obviously he still had 'faith' in Jesus to save him. Speaking further to Peter's feeling of unworthiness, *"Now when He had left speaking, He said unto Simon, Launch out into the deep, and let down your nets for draught. And Simon answering said unto Him, Master, we have toiled all the night, and have taken nothing: nevertheless at Thy word I will let down the net. And when they had this done, they enclosed a great multitude of fishes: and their net brake. And they beckoned unto their partners, which were in the other ship, that they should come and help them. And they came, and filled both the ships, so that they began to sink. When Simon Peter saw it, he fell down at Jesus' knees, saying, Depart from me; for I am a sinful man, O Lord. For he was astonished, and all that were with him, at the draught of the fishes which they had taken: And so was also James, and John, the sons of Zebedee, which were partners with Simon. And Jesus said unto Simon, Fear not; from hence forth thou shalt catch men."* (Luke 5:4-10) Thus, despite Peter's feeling of unworthiness, Jesus still chose him as a disciple. In fact, Jesus not only kept him as one of His disciples but said that the foundation of His church would be built upon him!

"For whatsoever is born of God overcometh the world: and this is the victory that overcometh the world, even our faith. Who is he that overcometh the world, but he that believeth that Jesus is the Son of God?" (1 John 5: 4-5) *"He that hath an ear, let him hear what the Spirit saith unto the churches; To him that overcometh will I give to eat of the tree of life, which is in the midst of the paradise of God."* (Revelation 2:7) *"To him that overcometh will I grant to sit with Me in My throne, even as I also overcame, and am*

set down with My Father in His throne." (Revelation 3:21) *"He that overcometh shall inherit all things; and I will be his God, and he shall be My son."* (Revelation 21:7). And what is to be overcome? *"For all that is in the world, the lust of the flesh, and the lust of the eyes, and the pride of life, is not of the Father, but is of this world."* (1 John 2:16)

Immortality or **SURVIVAL** into **ACTUAL REALITY** only comes by denying self, 'overcoming' the world through Jesus Christ and substituting the Will of God for yours, and that is the irony of Christianity. **You give up 'everything' to gain everything!**

*Some American corporations who moved to Mexico, for example, reportedly are blatantly dumping toxins into streams and are taking no efforts to avoid polluting the air. Even in the United States after the 1994 elections, it appeared, for a time, as if the politicians were going to 'cave in' to multi-national corporations and allow them to begin polluting our **own** air and water, **again**!

†It is, even after 2,000 years, hard for us to grasp that Jesus was a manifestation of God. Thus, He was God. God appeared at times in different forms or ways to Biblical man in the Old Testament. <u>God</u> is God; He can do anything and be anywhere and everywhere.

Chapter 24
Conclusion

There is a maturing process wherein the constant presence and love of God is increasingly felt. However, the natural man corrupts this process by reversing the notion of denying himself and, instead of exalting God, he exalts himself or some other human being. Man is not inherently good and this is so obvious when you really allow yourself to look around at the world, at history. Man has so corrupted God's **ACTUAL REALITY** ever since Eden that he is now on the verge of creating an increasingly thoroughgoing VIRTUAL REALITY.

Reason and logic are systems of thought that, in themselves, are limited. Even thought has its restrictions. Reason has many physical benefits, but it is a two-edged sword and has a treacherous downside that can supplant God. Man would never have been capable of 'sin' if he had not had the knowledge of the existence of good and evil. But humans, in their sojourn on earth, are on an odyssey to comprehend God and progress from a physical mortality to Spiritual immortality. This process not only goes beyond reason, but can be impeded by reason. Nevertheless, Darwin's 'evolution' cannot invalidate God, Freud's 'unconscious' cannot replace Satan and Einstein's 'relativity' cannot give mankind immortality.

Faith is opposed to conventional wisdom. All the 'wisdom' of the carnal mind is not of God and does not subject itself to the laws of God. Man's world is a counterfeit of God's and but a dim glimmer of what God can bring about. Jesus had a creed that would make this world an earthly paradise, if followed; but His creed was foolishness to 'learned' men, and one that they could never establish because of human nature's greed, lust and violence. Scientists 'know' that physical reality is based on mass and energy, which are no more real than the ephemeral bits and bites, ones and zeros of the computer age and cyberspace. Man's creations are illusions – no more than dreams caught in time, which, in turn, are merely constructs – a VIRTUAL REALITY, which will vanish.

Psychology is the study of the effects of the conversion of sensory input into perceptions that are products of each individual's experiences. Thus, each individual is living in a unique world, a world of illusion, because he creates his perceptions from his experiences – no matter how far they are from the 'norm'. Solipsism (a theory that the self is the only reality) may not be too far from the way things are in this physical world. Once carnal mind has enthroned perception as its ruling monitor and thus, walled itself off from the Spiritual, it becomes a prisoner of illusion, i.e., of the physical senses.

For those who do not look beyond the here and now and are 'lukewarm' to issues about life and meaning, i.e., those who don't delve into things or think things through, are in the category of not knowing that they don't know. Perhaps even more dangerous are those 'learned elite' who allow themselves to become impressed and prejudiced with and by their thinking to the degree that they believe they know it all and are not receptive or open to change and growth. Over-generalizing and over-simplifying, as well as over-complicating, create more problems than they solve.

The 'game' of life is as temporal and unreal as the VIRTUAL REALITY of an interactive computer-generated simulation of reality (cyberspace) utilizing head sets for sensual reception and data gloves for personal transmission. **ACTUAL REALITY** is **GOD'S REALITY** of which we are mostly ignorant. We do know the way there because Jesus showed us the Way, the Truth and the Life. God loved man so much that He entered part of His creation and walked among us as one of us, showing us how we should live by His example and His teachings. He did not show us the life or the world to come, but He did show us how to get there by accepting and living the Spiritual life and rejecting the carnal mind.

There is a cosmic struggle between the forces of Satan (evil), and God, who is good, over the soul of man. God is the life and light of man and yet, as Job says of certain evil men, *"They are of those that rebel against the light; they know not the ways thereof, nor abide in the paths thereof."* (Job 24:13) Men that do not believe in a living beneficent God, cannot see evidence of Him, nor hear His messages. They are living in limbo, killing, stealing, lying – in the dark, literally and figuratively. The more sophisticated and 'learned' are ruled by greed, lust and deceit, utilizing technological advances to manipulate populations and rule in 'great families' of banking, commerce and industry. (This is not to say all successful financial, industrial and service providers are evil. However, resisting evil becomes harder with greater acquisition of power or wealth.) These also are in the dark and, along with their less sophisticated brothers, are just as ignorant and deaf and blind to the truth, and the cosmic struggle. They give lip service to God, not in faith, but as a means to mislead the 'common man'. Men of faith can see and hear God's truth, but the cosmic struggle is beyond their ability to fix or change and even to really understand.

'Community' is a vital concept for the fruitful Christian life. We must be peaceable, law-abiding and loving to the best of our ability. This necessitates calling on God's Holy Spirit. Only through Christ can our weakness be turned into His strength. As God said, *"...Not by might, nor by power, but by My Spirit."* (Zecharias 4:6) To make the gift of faith real and a working paradigm in our lives is the basis for providing meaning and purpose to human lives. *"And He said unto me, My grace is sufficient for thee: for my strength is made perfect in weakness. Most gladly therefore will I rather glory in my infirmities, that the power of Christ may rest upon me."* (2 Corinthians 12:9)

The essence of anything, the idea or plan of something, comes before its existence. It is only after existence that functioning can begin and, not until after the process of functioning, can it be determined whether or not all is working according to plan. We humans must not only be, but must do, in order to be perfect. However, long before we were born, we were doomed to failure because of a flaw in our ancestor, and no amount of trying has ever been able to overcome that defect and be perfect (as far as we know) – until Jesus Christ. In this last stage of 'evolutionary' dealing with man, God has said we must just **be** – in Christ, He has done the doing. So our pride, our will and our self, must go and we, in faith, must accept what God has given us, what Christ has done for us. *"Neither pray I for these alone, but for them also which shall believe on Me through their word; That they all may be one; as Thou, Father, art in Me, and I in Thee, that they also may be one in Us: that the world may believe that Thou has sent Me. And the glory which Thou gavest Me I have given them; that they may be one, even as We are one: I in them, and Thou in Me, that they may be made perfect in one; and that the world may know that Thou hast sent Me, and hast loved them, as Thou hast loved Me."* (John 17:20-23)

Today, most people are not only unheeding to the message of the New Testament, but unmindful of it. Their difficulty in delaying gratification of their senses and the unacceptability of uncertainty make of them creatures dedicated to living for the moment, strictly in the here and now. We humans are spirits housed within the vehicle of our physical bodies. It is not because we are so dependent upon our five senses that we have become imprisoned within our bodies, but because we are becoming so increasingly concerned with the gratification of our senses. We, in essence, are children of the marriage of technology and industrialization, enslaved by the scientific advances which extend or enhance our sensual pleasures. The devil is in the distractions that erect a wall of virtuality against God's reality.

Only God can open our eyes and ears to the truth and so, if you understand even in part what the New Testament is saying, then you can assume that you have been called – according to the Bible. It is then up to you to grow spiritually. One can thus, become a believer, a saint or a reprobate. A 'saint' studies the Bible and progressively seeks to be obedient to the Holy Spirit as the driving motivation in his or her life. There is confirmation in his or her life by the manifestation of the fruits of the Spirit. On the other hand, a 'believer' acknowledges Jesus Christ as the Son of God and believes in Him as his or her Saviour, but is more consumed with daily living and trying to be a 'good' person rather than in being in tune with the Holy Spirit and studying to make himself or herself a 'workman' unto God. The reprobate rejects the message altogether.

Competition is okay up to a point, but when it becomes cut-throat and any means are justified by the end and the end is money, power or other worldly 'success', then it is evil. Too often in modern economies, to make a bigger profit is 'justification' enough for reducing work forces to the point where hard working and loyal people lose their homes and sometimes their families. It is also 'justification' to make shoddy products, to create sweat shops and to lie about their product or service. Ambition, competition and rivalry must be tempered. If it is not, it is not Christian.

To meditate on phrases from the Bible in times of need, sleeplessness or doubt can be very comforting and strengthening of hope and faith. To enable this facility, one needs to read in the Bible, especially in the New Testament and Psalms. The more familiar one becomes with the Bible, the more precious it becomes and the more one feels the presence of the Holy Spirit. For example, *"Take no thought for the morrow: for the morrow shall take thought for the things of itself."* (Matthew 6:34) *"And ye shall know the truth and the truth shall make you free."* (John 8:32) *"There is no fear in love; but perfect love casteth out fear: because fear hath torment. He that feareth is not made perfect in love."* (1 John 4:18) *"For God hath not given us the spirit of fear; but of power, and of love, and of a sound mind."* (2 Timothy 1:7) *"For he that will love life, and see good days, let him refrain his tongue from evil, and his lips that they speak no guile: Let him eschew evil, and do good; let him seek peace, and ensue it."* (1 Peter 3:10-11) *"But the fruit of the Spirit is love, joy, peace, longsuffering, gentleness, goodness, faith, Meekness, temperance: against such there is no law."* (Galatians 5:22-23) *"But without faith it is impossible to please Him: for he that cometh to God must believe that He is, and that He is a rewarder of them that diligently seek Him."* (Hebrews 11:6)

The Bible does not 'whitewash' its heroes. It tells it like it is and, in doing so, gives us hope because we make so many mistakes and fall back into doubt so easily. Even David, who is mentioned more than any other person in the Bible, committed a terrible sin, and yet, God 'put away' his sin! There is hope for even the worst of us if we allow God's love to come into our hearts, and this is possible through persistent battle against doubt to the point of increasingly having a living faith in Jesus Christ. We sin, but God welcomes us back, like a good father or mother would do to a recalcitrant child.

How important it is to get a sense of proportion regarding the extent and direness of evil and suffering in our world. It is urgent for our society to reorder its priorities. Christianity is an all or nothing faith. There is no leeway for lukewarmness. Time appears to be running out for our civilization unless we begin to see beyond physical, carnal existence. To lose your 'self' is to gain immortality. If we act like animals, look like animals and live like animals, we will die like animals. The mortal end will be the end. A 'believer' is still partly controlled by the illusion of sin, a 'saint' has dispelled the mirage of sin and a non-believer is still fast in the grip of Satan and the delusion of sin. We are not just animals, we are also spirits, and if we allow our spiritual mind to dominate and defeat our carnal mind, then the death of our physical bodies will be the beginning of Spiritual immortality with God.

It requires a leap of faith to get in touch with **ACTUAL REALITY**. Those who are undecided or lukewarm, those who have not committed cannot contrast their VIRTUAL REALITY with **GOD'S ACTUAL REALITY** because they have never made that leap of faith in Jesus Christ. Heaven can begin here and now; we can transcend our VIRTUAL REALITY or we can have a foretaste of hell while still on earth. I believe that hell can exist for any person, anywhere, anytime that he or she is without God.

The basic flaws and sources of mankind's difficulties have arisen and are maintained because of the inserting and promoting of self in place of God. Self is a construct and an artifact of Adam's fall. It is false and the basis of VIRTUAL REALITY. Love, gifted from God, through the gift of Christian faith, kept alive by hope, enabled by the Holy Spirit, is the secret of life immortal. Hope is of vital importance because our faith is often so tentative in the transition from being occupied with 'self' to that of being spiritually minded. Hope allows faith to become stronger so that love can become more and more part of our feeling, thinking and being.

Two opposing forces struggling for dominance in each human mind are spiritual and carnal. The outcome determines for every human being whether he dies as an animal without escaping Satan's hell or becomes a member of God's family forever. This is a cosmic battle. St. Paul gives an indication that God is not involved with the carnal life and so, whether one is wealthy or poor may have nothing to do with God's favor. In fact, prosperity and a lifestyle of the rich and famous would appear to be much more of a hindrance to spirituality than poverty or illness – Jesus alludes to this often.

Why is it with the magnificent human mind and all its accomplishment, there is not, nor has there ever been, a utopia established on earth? Much evidence exists for the presence of evil. That evil force, if it is not man, works through man and the route is through the human 'self'. The enemy of mankind is in his carnal mind, i.e., the 'self'. Despite the passage of recorded history, there is little evidence of the presence of Spiritually oriented humankind of the order that the New Testament urges. Our savior is Christ, our enemy is Satan and the 'SELF'. It is ironic that when you are involved with 'self', you eventually end up damning your 'self', which inappropriately but inevitably has become confused with your identity, your unique individuality, i.e., who you **are**, which is a terrible travesty of reality – a perversion. 'Self' not only blocks awareness of God but also causes confusion in the identity. 'Self' is false to the n'th degree and is Satan's trump ace to deceive mankind.

When faith is weak, focus on hope and know that God is and always will be there for you. Do not allow 'self' in its many subtle forms to enter: self doubt, self-esteem, self confidence, self image, selfishness, self-consciousness, self-centeredness. If you are in psychotherapy, and the therapist focuses on 'self', contest it and reject it. If that does not work, change therapists or find a minister who is dealing with **ACTUAL REALITY**. Break free of VIRTUAL REALITY before that illusion becomes a delusion. We must be able to distinguish our unique individuality from 'self'; 'self' and identity are not the same.

It is my conclusion that free love and free will are both of the same ilk. 'Will' and 'self' are of this physical, sensual world of VIRTUAL REALITY; they are not God given. Man was created without free will and without self-centeredness, in the perfection of his essence which God created in the first creation. Self and a will separate one from God and are of Satan and fallen man. Man is free to choose God's Will or to rebel and reject it, in which case he automatically chooses Satan's will and becomes Satan's – until and unless he repents. Human 'will' and 'self' are inextricably bound together; they are almost interchangeable. Each demands control and domination.

I truly think that the sooner one turns to Jesus in faith, the more noble and the more fulfilling life will be, not only in the hereafter, but in the here and now as well. It is hard for me to believe that a 'saint' will not have some reward over that of a 'believer' in our coming Spiritual lives. Be that as it may, there is no question in my mind that everyone who turns to Christ and struggles with faith, reaching that point where God's love is a real presence, begins to live in **ACTUAL REALITY** in the here and now. And that is a foretaste of glory.

St. Paul makes an interesting statement, if not a puzzling one, in his first letter to Timothy in the fourth chapter and the tenth verse as follows, *"For therefore we both labour and suffer reproach, because we trust in the living God, Who is the Saviour **of all men**, specially of those that believe."* (1 Timothy 4:10) One could read this to the effect that all men are saved eventually or somehow, but no matter what others may read into this, it certainly points out that we do not understand everything about God's plan for humans nor how or when it is to be accomplished. **It does give us all hope.** There may well be an order or a hierarchy in heaven, but undoubtedly different than any organizational hierarchy on earth, and most certainly one without envy, jealousy, strife or competition. **For there will be love.**

FAITH IS THE KEY.

I am quoting a poem by Francis Thompson where he writes, in poetic language, an allegorical memoir of his lost life. A stranger in a world that was not home to him and from which he hid, 'aided' much of his life by the drug, Laudanum. Despite his great talent, he was a derelict, a street person until finally 'rescued' toward the end of his life and taken in, given shelter and care. He turns to God in surrender and acceptance, as a Christian. Another poem reveals this as well, namely, his poem from *In No Strange Land*, titled "The Kingdom of God is Within You".

The Hound of Heaven

I fled Him, down the nights and down the days;
I fled Him, down the arches of the years;
I fled Him, down the labyrinthine ways
of my own mind; and in the midst of tears
I hid from Him, and under running laughter.
Up vistaed hopes I sped;
And shot, precipitated,
Adown Titanic glooms of chasmed fears,
From those strong Feet that followed, followed after,
But with unhurrying chase,
And unperturbed pace,
Deliberate speed, majestic instancy,
They beat – and a Voice beat
More instant than the Feet –
"All things betray thee, who betrayest Me,"

I pleaded, outlaw-wise,
By many a hearted casement, curtained red,
Trellised with intertwining, charities
(For, though I knew His love Who followed,
Yet was I sore adread
Lest, having Him, I must have naught beside);
But, if one little casement parted wide,

The gust of His approach would clash it to:
Fear wist not to evade, as Love wist to pursue,
Across the margent of the world I fled,
And troubled the gold gateways of the stars,
Smiting for shelter on their clanged bars;
Fretted to dulcet jars
And silvern chatter the pale ports o' the moon.
I said to Dawn: Be sudden-to Eve: Be soon;
With thy young skiey blossoms heap me over
From this tremendous Lover –
Float thy vague veil about me, lest He see!
I tempted all His servitors, but to find
My own betrayal in their constancy,
In faith to Him their fickleness to me,
Their traitorous trueness, and their loyal deceit,
To all swift things for swiftness did I sue;
Clung to the whistling mane of every wind,
But whether they swept, smoothly fleet,
The long savannahs of the blue;
Or whether, Thunder-driven,
They clanged his chariot 'thwart a heaven,
Plashy with flying lightnings round the spurn o' their feet: –
Fear wist not to evade as Love wist to pursue.
Still with unhurrying chase,
And unperturbed pace,
Deliberate speed, majestic instancy,
Came on the following Feet,
And a Voice above their beat;
"Naught shelters thee, who wilt not shelter Me."

I sought no more that after which I strayed
In face of man or maid;
But still within the little children's eyes
Seems something, something that replies,
They at least are for me, surely for me!

I turned me to them very wistfully;
But just as their young eyes grew sudden fair
With dawning answers there,
Their angel plucked them from me by the hair.
"Come then, ye other children, Nature's-share
With me" (said I) "your delicate fellowship;
Let me greet you lip to lip,
Let me twine with you caresses,
Wantoning
With our Lady-Mother's vagrant tresses,
Banqueting
With her in her wind-walled palace,
Underneath her azured dais,
Quaffing, as your taintless way is,
From a chalice
Lucent-weeping out of the dayspring."
So it was done:
I in their delicate fellowship was one –
Drew the bolt of Nature's secrecies.
I knew all the swift importings
On the willful face of skies;
I knew how the clouds arise
Spumed of the wild sea-snortings;
All that's born or dies
Rose and drooped with; made them shapers
Of mine own moods, or wailful or divine;
With them joyed and was bereaven.
I was heavy with the even,
When she lit her glimmering tapers
Round the day's dead sanctities.
I laughed in the morning's eyes.
I triumphed and I saddened with all weather,
Heaven and I wept together,
And its sweet tears were salt with mortal mine;

Against the red throb of its sunset-heart
I laid my own to beat,
And share commingling heat;
But not by that, by that, was eased my human smart.
In vain my tears were wet on Heaven's gray cheek.
For ah! we know not what each other says,
These things and I; in sound I speak –
Their sound is but their stir, they speak by silences.
Nature, poor stepdame, cannot slake my drouth;
Let her, if she would owe me,
Drop yon blue bosom – veil of sky, and show me
The breasts o' her tenderness;
Never did any milk of hers once bless
My thirsting mouth.
Nigh and nigh draws the chase,
With unperturbed pace,
Deliberate speed, majestic instancy;
And past those noised Feet
A Voice comes yet more fleet –
"Lo! naught contents thee, who content'st not Me."

Naked I wait Thy love's uplifted stroke!
My harness piece by piece Thou hast hewn from me,
And smitten me to my knee;
I am defenseless utterly.
I slept, methinks, and woke,
And, slowly gazing, find me stripped in sleep.
In the rash lustihead of my young powers,
I shook the pillaring hours
And pulled my life upon me; grimed with smears,
I stand amid the dust o' the mounded years –
My mangled youth lies dead beneath the heap.
My days have crackled and gone up in smoke,
Have puffed and burst as sun-starts on a stream.
Yea, faileth now even dream

The dreamer, and the lute the lutanist;
Even the linked fantasies, in whose blossomy twist
I swung the earth a trinket at my wrist,
Are yielding; cords of all too weak account
For earth with heavy griefs so overplused.
Ah! is Thy love indeed
A weed, albeit an amaranthine weed,
Suffering no flowers except its own to mount?
Ah! must –
Designer infinite! –
Ah! must Thou char the wood ere Thou canst limn with it?
My freshness spent its wavering shower i' the dust;
And now my heart is as a broken fount,
Wherein tear-drippings stagnate, spilt down ever
From the dank thoughts that shiver
Upon the sighful branches of my mind.
Such is; what is to be?
The pulp so bitter, how shall taste the rind?
I dimly guess what Time in mists confounds;
Yet ever and anon a trumpet sounds
From the hid battlements of Eternity;
Those shaken mists a space unsettle, then
Round the half-glimpsed turrets slowly wash again.
But not ere him who summoneth
I first have seen, enwound
With glooming robes purpureal, cypress-crowned;
His name I know, and what his trumpet saith.
Whether man's heart or life it be which yields
Thee harvest, must Thy harvest-fields
Be dunged with rotten death?

Now of that long pursuit
Comes on at hand the bruit;
That Voice is round me like a bursting sea:
"And is thy earth so marred,

Shattered in shard on shard?
Lo, all things fly thee, for thou fliest Me!
Strange, piteous, futile thing!
Wherefore should any set thee love apart?
Seeing none but I makes much of naught" (He said),
"And human love needs human meriting:
How hast thou merited –
Of all man's clotted clay the dingiest clot?
Alack, thou knowest not
How little worthy of any love thou art!
Whom wilt thou find to love ignoble thee
Save Me, save only Me?
All which I took from thee I did but take,
Not for thy harms,
But just that thou might'st seek it in My arms.
All which thy child's mistake
Fancies as lost, I have stored for thee at home:
Rise, clasp My hand, and come!"

Halts by me that footfall:
Is my gloom , after all,
Shade of His hand, oustretched caressingly?
"Ah, fondest, blindest, weakest,
I am He Whom thou seekest!
Thou dravest love from thee, who dravest Me."

Francis Thompson[16]

For Thompson, we see from the foregoing that Jesus Christ was the 'Hound of Heaven'. It is an artistic illumination of how we humans cheat ourselves in pursuing the delusion of VIRTUAL REALITY; being afraid to let go of what we 'have' (which is 'nothing') and, by faith, accepting all that God really offers us Spiritually in His **ACTUAL REALITY**.

I wish to close this chapter with an extended quote from *Workmen of God*, by Oswald Chambers.[1a] The following is excerpted from Chapter VI, The Worker Among Sick Souls, ". . .If our religion is only a religion of cheerfulness for the healthy-minded, it is no good for London, because more than half the people there, a great deal more than half, are not able to be cheerful, their minds and consciences and bodies are so twisted and tortured that exactly the opposite seems to be their portion. All the talking and preaching about healthy-mindedness, about cheering up and living in the sunshine will never touch that crowd. If all Jesus Christ can do is to tell a man he has to cheer up when he is miserable; if all the worker for God can do is to tell a man he has no business to have the 'blues' – I say if that is all Jesus Christ's religion can do, then it is a failure. But the wonder of our Lord Jesus Christ is just this, that you can face Him with any kind of men or women you like, and He can cure them and put them into a right relationship with God.(pages 59-60.)

". . .One word about the physical condition of people. There is a threshold to our nerves, that is, a place where the nerves begin to record. Some people's nerves do not record things as quickly as others. Some people have what is called the 'misery' threshold of nerves, the threshold where the nerves begin to record is much lower down than it is in other people. Take it in connection with sound; some people can sleep in a tremendous racket, noise makes not the slightest difference to them. The ear gathers up vibrations, and only when those vibrations are quick enough, do we hear. If the threshold of our hearing were lower, we should hear anything that makes waves in the atmosphere; we should hear the flowers grow. Everything that grows makes a motion in the atmosphere. The majority of us have a threshold that is high up, and we cannot hear unless there is sufficient vibration in the atmosphere. Get a nervous system where the threshold of nerves is low, and life is an abject torture to that one wherever he goes. What is the good of telling him to cheer up? There is a bigger problem there than we can touch. That one is in contact with forces which the majority of us know nothing about; he is tortured by things we never hear, tortured by things we never feel. Such people take a very gloomy view of life; they cannot help it.

"When a worker meets a soul like that, what is he going to do – preach the gospel of temperament, 'Cheer up and look on the bright side,' or preach Jesus Christ? 'The gospel of cheerfulness' is a catchword of the day – it may be all very well among people who are naturally cheerful, but what about folk who cannot be cheerful, who through no fault of their own have bodies, where the threshold of their nerves is so low down, that life is a misery? . . .These people will accept all you say about the need to receive His Spirit, but nothing happens; they do not cheer up. How are we going to bring Jesus Christ into contact with them?. . .

". . .There are only two religions that accept gloom as a fact (I mean by gloom, sin, anguish, and misery, the things that make people feel that life is not worth living), Buddhism and Christianity. Every other religion ignores it. This is the age of the gospel of cheerfulness. We are told to ignore sin, ignore the gloomy people, and yet more than half the human race is gloomy. Sum up your own circle of acquaintances, and then draw your inference. Go over the list, and before long you will have come across one who is gloomy, he has a 'sick' view of things, and you cannot alter that one. How are you going to get that oppression taken off? Tell him to take so many weeks' holiday by the sea? Take iron pills and tonics? No! Living in the peace and joy of God's forgiveness and favour is the only thing that will brighten up and bring cheerfulness to such a one. **Only when God takes a life in hand can there come deliverance** [my emphasis] from the 'blues', deliverance from fits of depression, discouragement and all such moods. The Scriptures are full of admonitions to rejoice, to praise God, to sing aloud for joy; but only when one has a cause to rejoice, to praise, and sing aloud, can these things truly be done from the heart.(pages 61-64.)

". . .Anguish is as real as joy; fired, jangled and tortured nerves are as real as nerves in order. Low threshold nerves, where everything is an exquisite misery, are as real as high threshold nerves where nothing is misery. Listen to this, they are Luther's own words:

"'I am utterly weary of life. I pray the Lord will come forthwith and carry me hence. Let Him come above all with His last judgement. I will stretch out my neck, the thunder will burst forth and I shall be at rest.' And having a necklace of white agates in his hand at the time, he added: 'O God, grant that it may come without delay. I would readily eat up this necklace today for the judgment to come tomorrow.' The Electress Dowager one day, when Luther was dining with her, said to him, 'Doctor, I wish you may live forty years to come.' 'Madam,' he replied, 'rather than live forty years more, I would give up my chance of Paradise.'

"That was Luther speaking at the end of his life. What produced the misery? He saw the havoc the Reformation had wrought. He did not see the good, – he was too near it.

"There was the same thing in Goethe's writings; in 1824, he writes, 'I will say nothing against the course of my existence, but at the bottom, it has been nothing but pain and burden, and I can affirm that, during the whole of my seventy-five years, I have not had four weeks of genuine well-being. It has been the perpetual rolling of a rock that must be raised up again.'

"Robert Louis Stevenson said that three hours out of every five, he was insane with misery. John Stuart Mill said that life was not worth living after you were a boy.

"This is not fiction, these are human facts. What does Christian Science do – ignores them! New Thought – ignores them! Mind Cure – ignores them! Jesus Christ opens our eyes to these facts. But here comes the difficulty: how am I to get Jesus Christ in contact with these sick souls?

"**In the first place, will you realize that you do not know how to do it?** [my emphasis] I want to lay that one principle down very strongly. If you think you know how to present Jesus Christ to a soul, you will never be able to do it. But if you will learn how to rely on the Holy Ghost, believing that Jesus Christ can do it, then I make bold to state that He will do it. If you get your little compartment of texts, and search them out and say, 'I know how to deal with this soul,' you will never be able to deal with it; but if you realize your absolute helplessness and say, 'My God, I cannot touch this life, I do not know where to begin, but I believe that Thou canst do it,' then you can do something.(pages 65-66.)

". . .Is not this the reason – you have been trying to find out what is wrong? God will never show you what is wrong; that is not your business. What He wants us to do is bring the case to Him: 'Lord, use my intercession as channel through which Thou canst reach that soul.' God grant that we may be so centered in Him that He can use us in that wonderful way."(page70.)

My conclusion is that we are to live in the joy of the Holy Ghost and to be receptive to the Love of God. Of God is different—more powerful and more accurate than our love to God or for God. Love is of and from God and is always, instantly, and constantly available — in Christ which is to say — unconditional, Christ is in our hearts through God's Grace and faith <u>when</u> we get out of our way, in other words, when we reject our carnal 'self' and our 'will'. For Christ has met all the preconditions and we are His, <u>Who enables</u> us to follow His truth, His Way and His Life.

Psalm 23

The Lord is my shepherd; I shall not want.
2 He maketh me to lie down in green pastures: He leadeth me beside still waters.
3 He restoreth my soul: He leadeth me in the paths of righteousness for His name's sake.
4 Yea, though I walk through the valley of the shadow of death, I will fear no evil: for Thou art with me; Thy rod and Thy staff they comfort me.
5 Thou preparest a table before me in the presence of mine enemies: Thou anointest my head with oil; my cup runneth over.
6 Surely goodness and mercy shall follow me all the days of my life: and I will dwell in the house of the Lord for ever.

Psalm 91

He that dwelleth in the secret place of the most High shall abide under the shadow of the Almighty.
2 I will say of the Lord, He is my refuge and my fortress: my God; in Him I will trust.
3 Surely He shall deliver thee from the snare of the fowler, and from the noisome pestilence.
4 He shall cover thee with His feathers, and under His wings shalt thou trust: His truth shall be thy shield and buckler.
5 Thou shalt not be afraid for the terror by night; nor for the arrow that flieth by day;
6 Nor for the pestilence that walketh in darkness; nor for the destruction that wasteth at noonday.
7 A thousand shall fall at thy side, and ten thousand at thy right hand; but it shall not come near thee.
8 Only with thine eyes shalt thou behold and see the reward of the wicked.

9 Because thou hast made the Lord, which is my refuge, even the Most High, thy habitation;
10 There shall no evil befall thee, neither shall any plague come near thy dwelling.
11 For He shall give His angels charge over thee, to keep thee in all thy ways.
12 They shall bear thee up in their hands, lest thou dash thy foot against a stone.
13 Thou shalt tread upon the lion and the adder: the young lion and the dragon shalt thou trample under feet.
14 Because he hath set his love upon Me, therefore will I deliver him: I will set him on high, because he hath known My name.
15 He shall call upon Me, and I will answer him: I will be with him in trouble; I will deliver him, and honor him.
16 With long life will I satisfy him, and show him My salvation.

One last quote to put an end to charges of polytheism.
"Endeavoring to keep the unity of the Spirit in the bond of peace. There is one body, and one Spirit, even as ye are called in one hope of your calling; One Lord, one faith, one baptism, One God and Father of all, Who is above all, and through all, and in you all." (Ephesians 4:3-6).

General Index

[Note: all **bolded** terms are major concepts within the text.]

Scriptural Index
NEW TESTAMENT

ACTS

COLOSSIANS

1 CORINTHIANS

2 CORINTHIANS

EPHESIANS

GALATIANS

HEBREWS

JAMES

JOHN

REVELATION

ROMANS

OLD TESTAMENT

Bibliography

1 Chambers, Oswald. *Biblical Psychology*. 1941, reprinted 1948: Butler & Tanner, Ltd. Distributed by Simpkin Marshall, Ltd., London. [*Biblical Psychology* by Oswald Chambers. Copyright 1962, 1995: Oswald Chambers Publ. Assn., Ltd. Used by permission of Discovery House Publ., Box 3566, Grand Rapids, MI 49501. Rights reserved.]

1a Chambers, Oswald. *Workmen of God*. 1937, reprinted 1953: Butler & Tanner, Ltd. Distributed by Marshall, Morgan, & Scott, Ltd., London. [*So I Send You/Workmen of God* by Oswald Chambers. Copyright 1937, 1993: Oswald Chambers Publ. Assn., Ltd. Used by permission of Discovery House Publ., Box 3566, Grand Rapids, MI 49501. Rights reserved.]

2 Ernst, Bruno. *The Magic Mirror of M.C. Escher*. 1985: Tarquin Publications, England.

3 Evans, M. Stanton. *The Theme is Freedom*. 1994: Regnery Publishing Inc., Washington, D.C.

4 Frum, David. *Dead Right*. 1994: Basic Books, New York.

5 Gardner Assoc. *Who's Who in the Bible*. 1994: The Reader's Digest Assoc., U.S.A.

6 Hammarskjold, Dag. *Markings*. Pages xv-xvi & 205; as translated by Leif Sjoberg and W. H. Auden.1964: Alfred A. Knopf, New York, N.Y.

7 Hayek, F. A. *The Road to Serfdom*. 1994: The University of Chicago Press, Chicago, Ill.

8 Howard, Philip K. *The Death of Common Sense*.1994: Random House, Inc., New York.

9 *I.B.M. Dictionary of Computing*, 1993: McGraw-Hill, Inc., New York.

10 Kierkegaard, Soren. *The Diary of Soren Kierkegaard*. 1960: Philosophical Library, Inc., New York. Translated from the Danish by Gerda M. Andersen.

11 Lynch, James J. *The Language of the Heart*. 1985: Basic Books, New York.

12 McDonald, Forrest. *The American Presidency*. 1994: University Press of Kansas, Lawrence, Kansas.

13 Olasky, Marvin. *The Tragedy of American Compassion*. 1992: Regnery Publishing Inc., Washington, D.C.

14 Strong, James. *The Exhaustive Concordance of the Bible*. 1894: Abington Books, New York.

15 Unger, Merrill F. *Unger's Bible Dictionary*. 1957: The Moody Bible Institute, Chicago, Ill.

16 Untermeyer, Louis. *A Treasury of Great Poems: English and American*. 1942: Simon and Schuster,New York.

Bruce P. Burns, Ph.D., is a clinical psychologist currently in private practice in Troy, residing in Bloomfield Hills, Michigan.

To order, send check to:

Bruce P. Burns, Ph.D.
P.O. Box 527
Bloomfield Hills, Michigan 48303-0527

or write to:

Proctor Publications
P.O. Box 2498
Ann Arbor, Michigan 48106-2498
(800) 343–3034

Single copies: $12.95 US for paperback, plus $2.50 shipping/handling. $21.95 US for hardcover, plus $2.95 shipping/handling. For additional copies, add .50 per copy for shipping.